FORWARD/COMMENTARY

The National Institute of Standards and Technology (NIST) is a measurement standards laboratory, and a non-regulatory agency of the **United States Department of Commerce**. Its mission is to promote innovation and industrial competitiveness. Founded in 1901, as the National Bureau of Standards, NIST was formed with the mandate to provide standard weights and measures, and to serve as the national physical laboratory for the United States. **With a** world-class measurement and testing laboratory encompassing a wide range of areas of computer science, mathematics, statistics, and systems engineering, NIST's cybersecurity program supports its overall mission to promote U.S. innovation and industrial competitiveness by advancing measurement science, standards, and related technology through research and development in ways that enhance economic security and improve our quality of life.

The need for cybersecurity standards and best practices that address interoperability, usability and privacy has been shown to be critical for the nation. NIST's cybersecurity programs seek to enable greater development and application of practical, innovative security technologies and methodologies that enhance the country's ability to address current and future computer and information security challenges.

The cybersecurity publications produced by NIST cover a wide range of cybersecurity concepts that are carefully designed to work together to produce a holistic approach to cybersecurity primarily for government agencies and constitute the best practices used by industry. This holistic strategy to cybersecurity covers the gamut of security subjects from development of secure encryption standards for communication and storage of information while at rest to how best to recover from a cyber-attack.

Why buy a book you can download for free?   **We print this so you don't have to.**

Some are available only in electronic media. Some online docs are missing pages or barely legible.

We at 4th Watch Publishing are former government employees, so we know how government employees actually use the standards. When a new standard is released, an engineer prints it out, punches holes and puts it in a 3-ring binder. While this is not a big deal for a 5 or 10-page document, many NIST documents are over 100 pages and printing a large document is a time-consuming effort. So, an engineer that's paid $75 an hour is spending hours simply printing out the tools needed to do the job. That's time that could be better spent doing engineering. We publish these documents so engineers can focus on what they were hired to do – engineering. It's much more cost-effective to just order the latest version from Amazon.com

If there is a standard you would like published, let us know. Our web site is www.usgovpub.com

Many of our titles are available as ePubs for Kindle, iPad, Nook, remarkable, BOOX, and Sony eReaders.

Why buy an eBook when you can access data on a website for free? HYPERLINKS

Yes, many books are available as a PDF, but not all PDFs are bookmarked? Do you really want to search a 6,500-page PDF document manually? Load our copy onto your Kindle, PC, iPad, Android Tablet, Nook, or iPhone (download the FREE kindle App from the APP Store) and you have an easily searchable copy. Most devices will allow you to easily navigate an ePub to any Chapter. Note that there is a distinction between a Table of Contents and "Page Navigation". Page Navigation refers to a different sort of Table of Contents. Not one appearing as a page in the book, but one that shows up on the device itself when the reader accesses the navigation feature. Readers can click on a navigation link to jump to a Chapter or Subchapter. Once there, most devices allow you to "pinch and zoom" in or out to easily read the text. (Unfortunately, downloading the free sample file at Amazon.com does not include this feature. You have to buy a copy to get that functionality, but as inexpensive as eBooks are, it's worth it.) Kindle allows you to do word search and Page Flip (temporary place holder takes you back when you want to go back and check something). Visit **www.usgovpub.com** to learn more.

NISTIR 8011
Volume 3

Automation Support for Security Control Assessments

Software Asset Management

Kelley Dempsey
Paul Eavy
Nedim Goren
George Moore

This publication is available free of charge from:
https://doi.org/10.6028/NIST.IR.8011-3

National Institute of
Standards and Technology
U.S. Department of Commerce

NISTIR 8011
Volume 3
Automation Support for Security Control Assessments

Software Asset Management

Kelley Dempsey
Nedim Goren
Computer Security Division
Information Technology Laboratory

Paul Eavy
Federal Network Resilience Division
Department of Homeland Security

George Moore
Johns Hopkins University
Applied Physics Laboratory

This publication is available free of charge from:
https://doi.org/10.6028/NIST.IR.8011-3

December 2018

U.S. Department of Commerce
Wilbur L. Ross, Jr., Secretary

National Institute of Standards and Technology
Walter Copan, NIST Director and Under Secretary of Commerce for Standards and Technology

National Institute of Standards and Technology Interagency Report 8011 Volume 3
210 pages (December 2018)

This publication is available free of charge from:
https://doi.org/10.6028/NIST.IR.8011-3

Comments on this publication may be submitted to:

National Institute of Standards and Technology
Attn: Computer Security Division, Information Technology Laboratory
100 Bureau Drive (Mail Stop 8930) Gaithersburg, MD 20899-8930
Email: sec-cert@nist.gov

All comments are subject to release under the Freedom of Information Act (FOIA).

Reports on Computer Systems Technology

The Information Technology Laboratory (ITL) at the National Institute of Standards and Technology (NIST) promotes the U.S. economy and public welfare by providing technical leadership for the Nation's measurement and standards infrastructure. ITL develops tests, test methods, reference data, proof-of-concept implementations, and technical analyses to advance the development and productive use of information technology. ITL's responsibilities include the development of management, administrative, technical, and physical standards and guidelines for the cost-effective security and privacy of other than national security related information in federal systems.

Abstract

The NISTIR 8011 volumes each focus on an individual information security capability, adding tangible detail to the more general overview given in NISTIR 8011 Volume 1, and providing a template for transition to a detailed, NIST guidance-based automated assessment. This document, Volume 3 of NISTIR 8011, addresses the Software Asset Management (SWAM) information security capability. The focus of the SWAM capability is to manage risk created by unmanaged or unauthorized software on a network. Unmanaged or unauthorized software is a target that attackers can use as a platform from which to attack components on the network.

Keywords

actual state; assessment; authorization boundary; automation; capability; continuous diagnostics and mitigation; dashboard; defect; desired state specification; firmware; information security continuous monitoring; ISCM; inventory management; malicious code; malware; mitigation; mobile code; ongoing assessment; root cause analysis; security capability; security control; security control item; software; software asset management; software file; SWID tag; whitelisting.

Acknowledgments

The authors, Kelley Dempsey and Ned Goren of the National Institute of Standards and Technology (NIST), Paul Eavy of the Department of Homeland Security, and Dr. George Moore of the Applied Physics Laboratory at Johns Hopkins University, wish to thank their colleagues who reviewed drafts of this document and provided valuable input, including Nathan Aileo, Ujwala Arikatla, Mark Bunn, Jim Foti, John Groenveld, Susan Hansche, Blair Heiserman, Frank Husson, Mike Ko, Alan McClelland, Susan Pagan, David Waltermire, and Kimberly Watson. The authors also gratefully acknowledge and appreciate the comments and contributions made by government agencies, private organizations, and individuals in providing direction and assistance in the development of this document.

Table of Contents

List of Figures

List of Tables

Executive Summary

The National Institute of Standards and Technology (NIST) and the Department of Homeland Security (DHS) have collaborated to produce this report which describes a process that automates the test assessment method described in NIST Special Publication (SP) 800-53A for the security controls catalogued in SP 800-53. The process is consistent with the Risk Management Framework as described in SP 800-37 and the Information Security Continuous Monitoring (ISCM) guidance in SP 800-137. The multi-volume NIST Interagency Report 8011 (NISTIR 8011) has been developed to provide information on automation support for ongoing assessment. NISTIR 8011 describes how ISCM facilitates automated ongoing assessment to provide near real-time security-related information to organizational officials on the security posture of individual systems and the organization as a whole.

NISTIR 8011 Volume 1 includes a description of *ISCM Security Capabilities*—groups of security controls working together to achieve a common purpose. The subsequent NISTIR 8011 volumes are capability-specific volumes. Each volume focuses on one specific ISCM information security capability in order to (a) add tangible detail to the more general overview given in NISTIR 8011 Volume 1; and (b) provide a template for the transition to detailed, standards-based automated assessments.

This publication, Volume 3 of NISTIR 8011, addresses the information security capability known as Software Asset Management (SWAM). The focus of the SWAM capability is to manage risk created by unmanaged or unauthorized software that are on a managed network. When software is unmanaged or unauthorized, they are vulnerable because the software files may be forgotten or unidentified. Moreover, when vulnerabilities are discovered on such software, responsibility to respond to the consequent risk is not assigned. As a result, the presence of unmanaged and unauthorized software means that devices are targets that attackers can use as a persistent platform from which to attack components on the network.

A well-designed SWAM program helps to:

- prevent compromised software from being installed or staying deployed on the network;
- prevent attackers from gaining a foothold;
- prevent attacks from becoming persistent; and
- restore required and authorized software as needed.

Automated ongoing assessment helps verify that software asset management is working by applying defect checks to test the effectiveness of the SWAM capability and the security controls that support the SWAM capability.

This volume outlines detailed step-by-step processes to meet the needs of a specific assessment target network and apply the results to the assessment of all authorization boundaries on that network. A process is also provided to implement the assessment (diagnosis) and response. Automated testing related to the controls for SWAM, as outlined herein, is consistent with other NIST guidance.

It has not been obvious to security professionals how to automate testing of other than technical controls. This volume documents a detailed assessment plan to assess the effectiveness of controls related to authorizing and assigning software to be managed. Included are specific tests that form the basis for such a plan, how the tests apply to specific controls, and the kinds of resources needed to conduct the assessment and use the assessment results to mitigate defects found. For SWAM, it can be shown that the assessment of 92.6 percent[1] of determination statements for controls in the SP 800-53 Low-Medium-High baselines can be fully or partially automated.

The methods outlined here for automated, ongoing assessment are designed to provide objective, timely, and complete identification of security defects related to SWAM at a lower cost than manual assessment methods. Using this defect information can drive the most efficient and effective remediation of the worst security defects found.

This volume assumes the reader is familiar with the concepts and ideas presented in the Overview (NISTIR 8011, Volume 1). Terms and acronyms used herein that are common to multiple capabilities are defined in Volume 1 Appendix B (glossary) and Appendix C respectively. Similarly, references used herein that are common to multiple capabilities are provided in Volume 1 Appendix A.

---

[1] Derived from the Control Allocation Tables (CAT) in this volume. With respect to security controls selected in the SP 800-53 Low-Medium-High baselines that support the SWAM capability, 75 of 81 determination statements (92.6%) can be fully or partially automated.

1. Introduction

1.1 Purpose and Scope

The purpose of the National Institute of Standards (NIST) Interagency Report (NISTIR) 8011 Volume 3 is to provide an operational approach for automating the ongoing assessment of NIST Special Publication (SP) 800-53[2] security controls related to the Information Security Continuous Monitoring (ISCM)-defined security capability of *Software Asset Management* (SWAM) that is consistent with the principles outlined in NISTIR 8011 Volume 1.[3]

The scope of this report is limited to security controls and control items that are implemented to manage the download, installation, and execution of unauthorized and malicious software (malware).[4] In this case, *malware* refers to known and unknown malicious code, including software that executes a zero-day attack.

1.2 Target Audience

The target audience for this volume, because it is focused on SWAM, is of special relevance to those who authorize, download, install and/or execute software. However, it is also of value to others to help understand the risks software may be imposing on other assets.

1.3 Organization of this Volume

Section 2 provides an overview of the SWAM capability to clarify both scope and purpose and provides links to additional information specific to the SWAM capability. Section 3 provides detailed information on the SWAM defect checks and how the defect checks automate assessment of the effectiveness of SP 800-53 security controls that support the SWAM capability. Section 3 also provides artifacts that can be used by an organization to produce an automated security control assessment plan for most of the control items supporting Software Asset Management.

---

[2] Joint Task Force Transformation Initiative, Security and Privacy Controls for Information Systems and Organizations, (2013), (National Institute of Standards and Technology, Gaithersburg, MD), NIST Special Publication (SP) 800-53, https://doi.org/10.6028/NIST.SP.800-53r4.

[3] Dempsey K., et al (2017) Automation Support for Security Control Assessments: Overview (National Institute of Standards and Technology, Gaithersburg, MD), NIST Interagency Report (IR) 8011 Volume 1, https://doi.org/10.6028/NIST.IR.8011-1.

[4] Malware, also known as malicious code, refers to a software program that is covertly inserted into another software program with the intent to destroy data, run destructive or intrusive software programs, or otherwise compromise the confidentiality, integrity, or availability of the victim's data, applications, or operating system. Source: Souppaya M., Scarfone K., (2013) (National Institute of Standards and Technology, Gaithersburg, MD), Guide to Malware Incident Prevention and Handling for Desktops and Laptops, NIST Special Publication (SP) 800-83, https://doi.org/10.6028/NIST.SP.800-83r1.

1.4 Interaction with Other Volumes in this NISTIR

Volume 1 of this NISTIR (Overview) provides a conceptual synopsis of using automation to support security control assessment and provides definitions and background information that facilitate understanding of the information in this and other capability-specific volumes.

This volume assumes the reader is familiar with the concepts and ideas presented in the Overview (NISTIR 8011, Volume 1). Terms and acronyms used herein that are common to multiple capabilities are defined in Volume 1 Appendix B (glossary) and Appendix C respectively. Similarly, references used herein that are common to multiple capabilities are provided in Volume 1 Appendix A.

The SWAM capability identifies software that is being placed or executed on hardware in the target network. SWAM supports other ISCM capabilities by providing the full census of software which can be used to check for other defects such as configuration settings (configuration setting management capability) and patches (vulnerability management capability).

SWAM is in turn supported by other ISCM capabilities such as the Privilege and Account Management capability (PRIV)[5] for implementation as discussed further in Section 2.6.1.

The Boundary Management capability (BOUND) is designed to prevent the insertion of unauthorized software into any device within the assessment boundary from outside the boundary. In contrast, the SWAM capability focuses on detecting and removing, or denying execution of all unauthorized or unmanaged software; however, some SWAM tools can also block unauthorized software from being installed on the device. For example, email filters attempt to block delivery of malicious emails, which frequently contain malware. Network level antivirus scanners have a similar function. Detonation Chambers (See SP 800-53, control SC-44) can be used on software entering the network, to look for actions that might be malicious, by watching behavior of that software in an isolated environment. Detonation chambers can thereby sometimes detect zero-day attacks if equipped to look for patterns of malicious behavior as discussed further toward the end of Section 2.3.

It may appear that some software related controls are, erroneously, not included here. However, not all software-related controls are covered in SWAM. SWAM focuses on software authorization. Other aspects of software are addressed in other ISCM capabilities, for example: Configuration Settings Management (CSM) addresses software configurations; Vulnerability Management (VULN) addresses vulnerability management (Common Vulnerabilities and Exposures (CVE) and Common Weakness Enumeration CWE)) and includes patching needed to address security issues (as opposed to patching needed for functionality issues which is addressed by SWAM); and BOUND addresses movement of unauthorized software into the network through telecommunications, etc.

---

[5] See Volume One for a discussion of ISCM capabilities.

2. Software Asset Management (SWAM) Capability Definition, Overview, and Scope

Software Asset Management recognizes that target network devices with unauthorized software[6] are likely to be vulnerable. External and internal attackers search for and exploit such software, either for what the software itself can offer, or as a platform from which to persist on the network or to attack other assets. By removing or preventing execution of unauthorized or unmanaged software, SWAM helps reduce the probability that attackers find and exploit software.

A key attack vector is to place (or replace) software on a device in order to perform malicious activities. Such software, called malware, can support exfiltration of data (compromising confidentiality), changing of data (compromising integrity), disruption of operations (compromising availability) and/or establishment of remote command and control over the device to more flexibly perform malicious activity at the will of the attacker. Removing unauthorized or unmanaged software from devices, or blocking its execution, can reduce the success rate of malware attacks.

Two Aspects of Software Asset Management

In a broader context, software asset management (SAM) is a business practice that includes purchasing, deploying, maintaining, using, and disposing of software applications.

In NISTIR 8011, software asset management (SWAM) is specifically focused on making informed decisions about the software authorized to be present on each device, given business need and security risk, and then enforcing the authorizations.

2.1 SWAM Capability Description

The Software Asset Management capability provides an organization visibility into the software operating on its network(s) so it can manage and defend itself. The SWAM capability focuses on making and enforcing software authorization decisions, balancing business need with security risk, and providing a view of software management responsibility that helps prioritize identified defects and facilitate risk response decisions (e.g., mitigation or acceptance) by the responsible party.

SWAM identifies software that is present on the network (the *actual state*) and compares it with the *desired state* software inventory to determine if the software present is authorized. The SWAM capability is focused on ensuring that all software authorized to be installed on target

---

[6] Unauthorized software is software that has not been assessed and authorized to be installed on target network devices as part of an overall system authorization process or individually if the software was installed after the initial system authorization. The organization may also consider implementing a process to deauthorize old software versions as new versions are authorized (see SWAM-L07).

network devices is fully identified and that an appropriate installation/execution control policy is applied.

In general, software authorization decisions can be expressed and enforced in one of two ways:

1. Software whitelisting[7] (deny-all, permit-by-exception) blocks all software unless explicitly approved in a *software whitelist*.
2. Software blacklisting (allow-all, deny-by exception) blocks only software specifically prohibited (a *software blacklist*) and allows all other software.

A whitelist or blacklist is a product of the authorization process. Blacklisting and whitelisting are inseparable from authorization. Supporting blacklisting and whitelisting are a set of informed decisions made about what software to authorize—considering both business need for the software and security risk introduced by the software.

Attacks can come from previously unknown malware (aka zero-day attacks). Note that software blacklisting[8] has effectively *no* impact on zero-day attacks because malware makers can make minor variations to software that evade blacklisting, thus allowing the attack to proceed. Conversely, software *whitelisting can* prevent zero-day attacks since whitelisting allows only explicitly approved software to execute.

Most software whitelisting implementations divide software into three categories:

1. Known good (allowed) software (such as a pre-approved whitelist)
2. Known bad software (such as a list of software that is *not* to be approved, similar to a blacklist, used to restrict the range of software that is whitelisted).
3. Other software, not yet assessed for whitelist eligibility (a *graylist*).[9]

---

[7] Software whitelisting is a deny-all, permit-by-exception strategy that only allows software to install, run, etc. by exception (i.e., if it is specified in an authorized software list as per NIST SP 800-53, CM-7(5)).

[8] As this volume is being written, blacklisting is not selected as a viable software authorization strategy for the low, moderate, or high baselines in the draft of NIST SP 800-53 Revision 5.

[9] A graylist is a list of discrete entities that have not yet been established as benign or malicious; more information is needed to move graylist items onto a whitelist or a blacklist. Source: Sedgewick A., et al (2015) Guide to Application Whitelisting (National Institute of Standards and Technology, Gaithersburg, MD), NIST Special Publication (SP) 800-167. https://doi.org/10.6028/NIST.SP.800-167, p. 2.

Note on Implementation of Application Whitelisting/Blacklisting

This NISTIR proposes automated defect checks for software asset management, some of which (SWAM-F01 through SWAM-F03) are used to test approaches to *software whitelisting* that are currently in common use. Use of a different approach might call for development of a modified foundational defect check to test that approach, as the organization is expected to deploy defect checks that match the approach to whitelisting or blacklisting actually used. There are a range of options for implementing software whitelisting, each with its own associated strengths and disadvantages, as described in detail in NIST SP 800-167.[10] Each organization is expected to conduct its own analysis and decide which variant of whitelisting or blacklisting is needed to manage risk effectively. Note that whitelisting methods are evolving—whitelisting is already a standard feature in most of the popularly used operating systems—so vigilance is required to ensure that new methods and options are considered as they appear and adopted as appropriate.

Organizations just beginning to whitelist may have a large quantity of software on the graylist. Some organizations may choose to temporarily allow (whitelist) the graylisted software. Others may block software on the graylist until the software is evaluated and approved. In either case, management of unassessed graylist software is an important task that may require a large amount of resources, especially in large or complex organizations.

In practice, organizations consider the following when whitelisting a software product:

1. **Whether to use whitelisting technologies built into available operating systems (OSs)**. As of this writing, most OSs have application control technologies, and software vendors continually improve the functionality of the technologies in new versions. When such improvements are made, organizations may leverage the new OS releases to limit or further restrict applications to develop a cleaner, more streamlined whitelist. A relevant feature for consideration is whether the OS version provides a trust repository of data on known good and known bad products and software files, and whether the repository is kept current.

2. **Maintaining different whitelists for different device sets**. For example, certain software might only appear on whitelists for specific types of components such as file servers, database servers, or end user devices. Similarly, the common operating system or the default email client used by an organization does not require a decision on each device, but appears on all whitelists maintained by an organization. Known malware, meanwhile, does not appear on *any* whitelist.

3. **Whitelisting in phases**. An organization might choose to implement whitelisting in software environments with predictable software turnover rates first, perhaps choosing those sets of devices under centrally managed desktops. Or, an organization might choose high-risk environments with high impact baseline control needs first. Organizations might schedule environments with many non-standard, low-risk or rapidly changing software components near the end of the whitelisting implementation.

---

[10] Sedgewick A., et al (2015) Guide to Application Whitelisting (National Institute of Standards and Technology, Gaithersburg, MD), NIST Special Publication (SP) 800-167, https://doi.org/10.6028/NIST.SP.800-167.

4. **Testing**. Monitoring or auditing mode, available in most whitelisting technologies, allows software managers to estimate the impact on resources before enforcing whitelisting. Monitoring allows planning for resource requirements in advance of actual implementation.

5. **Attributes**. Increasingly, organizations are implementing whitelisting products that support more granular whitelisting attributes, such as Software Identification (SWID) tags.[11] In the *Guide to Application Whitelisting* (2015), the authors note:

> *Choosing attributes is largely a matter of achieving the right balance of security, maintainability, and usability. Simpler attributes such as file path, filename, and file size should not be used by themselves unless there are strict access controls in place to tightly restrict file activity, and even then there are often significant benefits to pairing them with other attributes. A combination of digital signature/publisher and cryptographic hash techniques generally provides the most accurate and comprehensive application whitelisting capability, but usability and maintainability requirements can put significant burdens on the organization.*

The whitelisting/blacklisting strategy used in the ISCM process (as adapted for each agency) provides insight into what portion of the actual software assets are included in the desired state, and of those, how many have an assigned manager identified.

---

[11] Waltermire D., et al (2016), Guidelines for the Creation of Interoperable Software Identification (SWID) Tags (National Institute of Standards and Technology, Gaithersburg, MD), NIST Interagency Report (NISTIR) 8060, https://csrc.nist.gov/publications/detail/nistir/8060/final.

2.2 SWAM Attack Scenarios and Desired Result

NISTIR 8011 uses an attack step model to summarize the six primary steps of cyber attacks that SP 800-53 controls work together to block or delay. The *SWAM* security capability is intended to block or delay attacks only at the attack steps addressed in Figure 1: SWAM Impact on an Attack Step Model and Table 1: SWAM Impact on an Attack Step Model.

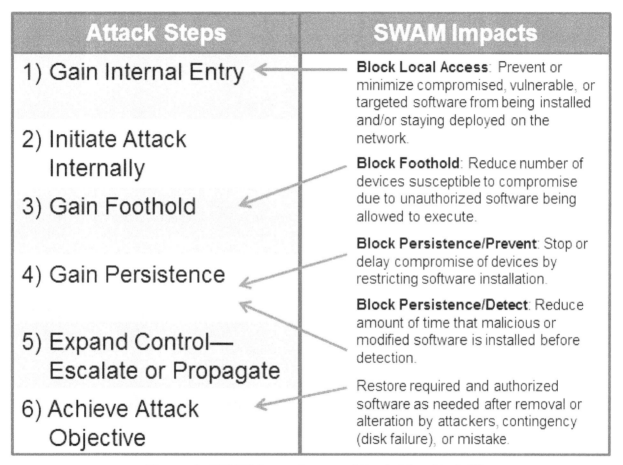

Figure 1: SWAM Impact on an Attack Step Model[12]

---

[12] The attack steps shown in Figure 1 apply only to adversarial attacks. (See NISTIR 8011, Volume 1, Section 3.2.)

Table 1: SWAM Impact on an Attack Step Model

Attack Step Name	Attack Step Purpose (General)	Capability-Specific Examples
1) Gain Internal Entry	The attacker is outside the target boundaries and seeks entry. Examples include: spear phishing email sent; distributed denial of service (DDoS) attack against .gov initiated; unauthorized person attempts to gain physical access to restricted facility.	Block Local Access: Prevent or minimize compromised, vulnerable, or targeted software from entering or being stored on the network or devices in a way that would allow installation or execution.
3) Gain Foothold	The attacker has gained entry to the assessment object and achieves enough compromise to gain a foothold, but without persistence. Examples include: unauthorized user successfully logs in with authorized credentials; browser exploit code successfully executed in memory and initiates call back; person gains unauthorized access to server room.	Block Foothold: Reduce number of devices susceptible to compromise due to unauthorized software being allowed to execute.
4) Gain Persistence	The attack has gained a foothold on the object and now achieves persistence. Examples include: malware installed on host that survives reboot or log off; basic input/output system (BIOS) or kernel modified; new/privileged account created for unauthorized user; unauthorized person issued credentials/allowed access; unauthorized personnel added to access control list (ACL) for server room.	Block Persistence/Prevent: Stop or delay compromise of devices by restricting software installation. Block Persistence/Detect: Reduce amount of time that malicious or compromised software is installed or remains active before detection and removal.
6) Achieve Attack Objective	The attacker achieves an objective. Loss of confidentiality, integrity, or availability of data or system capability. Examples include: exfiltration of files; modification of database entries; deletion of file or application; denial of service; disclosure of personally identifiable information (PII).	Restore required and authorized software as needed, after being removed or altered by attackers, contingency (disk failure), or by mistake.

Other examples of traceability among requirement levels. While Table 1 shows SWAM impacts on example attack steps, it is frequently useful to observe traceability among other sets of requirements. To examine such traceability, see Table 2: Traceability among Requirement Levels. To reveal traceability from one requirement type to another, look up the cell in the matching row and column of interest and click on the link.

Table 2: Traceability among Requirement Levels

	Example Attack Steps	Capability	Sub-Capability/ Defect Check	Control Items
Example Attack Steps		Figure 1 Table 1	Table 6	Appendix A
Capability	Figure 1 Table 1		Table 6	Section 3.3[a]
Sub-Capability/ Defect Check	Table 6	Table 6		Section 3.2[b]
Control Items	Appendix A	Section 3.3[a]	Section 3.2[b]	

[a] Each level-four section (e.g., 3.3.1.1) is a control item that supports this capability.
[b] Refer to the table under the heading *Supporting Control Items* within each defect check.

2.3 Assessment Objects Protected and Assessed by SWAM

As noted in Section 1.1, the assessment objects directly managed and assessed by the SWAM capability are software files and software products. However, the following clarification is relevant:

Software (code), as used here, includes a range of assets that might not always be thought of as software. Such software assets include:

- Installed software files and products listed in the operating system software database[13] (e.g., Windows registry, Linux package manager);
- Software files and products residing on a hard drive, but not listed in the operating system database;
- Mobile code;[14]
- Firmware, if it can be modified[15] (usually includes the BIOS); and
- Code in memory (which could be modified in place).

---

[13] Virtual machines are included in the operating system software database.
[14] Mobile code consists of software programs or parts of programs obtained from remote systems, transmitted across a network, and executed on a local system without explicit installation or execution by the recipient.
[15] Modifiable firmware is treated as software.

Note: Software includes all software on the system. The term *software* is not limited to business software, and also includes, for example, operating system software and security software (e.g., firewalls, white-listing software, configuration management tools, vulnerability scanners, etc.). The term *software* also includes shared code used by a product (e.g., dynamic link libraries (DLLs), other shared libraries, etc.). Appendix G reflects the relationship between configuration management controls and SWAM-related control items.

Each of the above types of software may require different controls to effectively prevent the execution of malicious software.

Software files can be stored on a device's mass storage, loaded into memory, and executed. [See Figure 4]; or software files can be mobile code obtained from a website.

Software files can be authoritatively identified by a message digest[16] computed from the software file. If an adversary tampers with the file, the tampering can be objectively and accurately confirmed by viewing the resulting change to the message digest.

Mobile code can be trusted based on the trust level assigned to any digital signature applied to the mobile code.

Files that include executable code are also software files (e.g., explicit executables, shared libraries, executable scripts, extensible stylesheet language (XSL) templates, documents that include macros that mix information with code). Because the files that include the executable code may change frequently, it is incumbent on the organization to identify and protect such files from unauthorized changes and to protect the system from files containing unauthorized changes, for example via use of a digital signature from a trusted source.

Figure 2: Definition and Discussion of *Software File* for SWAM

Software Products are collections of software files (generally sold as a unit) that work together to provide user functionality.

Examples of software products are operating systems (e.g., Apple IOS 11), office products (e.g., Microsoft Office), utilities (e.g., a database management system such as Oracle), or drivers that come with devices such as printers, scanners, monitors, etc.

A software product frequently has multiple versions. The versions include not only major versions (such as Oracle 12C), but also specific releases within versions, or minor versions, (such as 12.2) and the specific patches that may be applied to that release.

A unique product has the identical collection of software files with the same digital fingerprints as any other instance of that product. Any change in the files could be malicious.

Figure 3: Definition and Discussion of *Software Products* for SWAM

---

[16]A message digest results from applying a cryptographic hash function to an executable or file. The executable or file is the *message*, and the result of the computation is the *digest*. A message digest is also known as a *cryptographic hash value* or *digital fingerprint*.

Installed software files for software products may be shared by several other products as is notably true for shared library software files. An update to any one of the files for a product may update the shared library used by other products. Given the definition of a unique software product above—as a collection of software files with the same digital fingerprints—changing the shared library changes each of the affected products into a different product.

Software uninstallers may also leave some residue of a product behind on devices. For example, the uninstaller might not delete certain software files in shared libraries (because the files could potentially be used by another product). Since it is a common exploit to insert malware into files that are already included in a whitelisted product (e.g., by modifying an approved software product to load malware), risk is increased by software file residue from software product deinstallation. The file residue might not be detectable when using product-level whitelisting if the product-level whitelisting does not use message digests; however, software file residue may be detected by file-level whitelisting using message digests since when the modified software file attempts to load, its modified message digest is detected and execution is prevented.

Instances where software files and products are missing from the operating system software database occur because some software products do not require formal installation. The software files and products are simply copied to the device's mass storage, and then executed without creating software database entries.

In software approval processes, the focus is on whitelisting/blacklisting[17] of software *products* or software *files*. Because software products may be difficult to identify, focusing on software files is often more reliable. Identifying software at the product level (typically done via operating system software database entries) is significantly less reliable than identifying the product with a digital fingerprint for all files contained in the installation. However, it is still hard to identify the product (except probabilistically) because:

- The same *product*, even the same product *version*, might contain different files with different digital fingerprints, due to:
    - Differences in installation media;
    - Differences in installation options;
    - Subsequent patching of the product;
    - Subsequent patching of other products, e.g., that affect a shared DLL;
    - Attacker action that modifies a product file; or
    - Execution of an uninstalled file, not related to a registered product.

- When products are removed or upgraded, it is possible that not all software files are removed, as installers might not remove them fearing that particular files are still needed by other products. Such software files would remain subject to exploitation.

However, an organization that receives a product from a custom development team and/or a commercial off-the-shelf (COTS) supplier can register the contained (trusted) software files, and

---

[17] Whitelisting/blacklisting tools (and other utilities) might require execution of software agents on each device. The organization might find that collectively the software agents have some performance impact on the device. The overall selection of agents and configuration of agent behavior can be adjusted to allow adequate business performance by each device. See NIST SP 800-167 for more information on considerations for software whitelisting.

thereby reliably track whether exactly that specific version and patch level of the software is what has been installed.

Recognizing that software whitelisting at the product level is unreliable, the following four provisions can provide the needed reliability to software whitelisting at the executable file level using digital fingerprints:

1. **An *authoritative* directory of trusted software files (trusted repository)**. A trusted repository is developed by obtaining digital fingerprints from software files obtained as near to the trusted source as possible. The source might be a commercial software provider or an in-house custom software operation. When using open-source code, an authoritative directory might be more difficult to obtain, but can still be addressed by carefully examining the source code for the presence of CWEs and resolving issues found internally before trusting the code.

2. **A means to compute digital fingerprints and register trusted software not included in the vendor's trust repository.**

3. **Software files received as digitally-signed files from trusted sources**. If the code is mobile code, digital signing is an imperative (except perhaps on isolated disposable virtual machines). If mobile code is allowed, the trust can be established dynamically, based on the signature of the trusted source.

4. **Whitelisting software loaded near the *root* of the operating system (OS).** Whitelisting software loaded near the root of the OS blocks or requires permission to download, load-in-memory, and/or execute software that is not whitelisted.

Generally, a good software whitelisting product has all of capabilities (1), (2), (3), and (4), and supports automatic trust based on signature and/or identity of those who install the software.

It is important to note that SWID tags can make the process of identifying software products more deterministic by tagging products independent of the installation method and any associated patches.

As a result of the definition of software products, the use of shared files, and the ability to load software that is not inventoried in the operating system software database, it is very difficult to know what software products are on a device. Also, controlling software inventory based on software products listed in the operating system software database is highly unreliable, especially when compared to controlling software inventory based on digital fingerprints for software files. However, using software whitelisting with features 1 to 4, even while ignoring the operating system software database, resolves the unreliability issues.

Mobile code is distinguished by the fact that rather than being loaded from the device's mass storage, it is loaded at the time of use from the larger network (typically via a website). The code is managed externally, and may change frequently, rendering the device incapable of computing a valid digital fingerprint for the mobile code, and thus requiring other means to validate the code. Requiring the mobile code to be digitally signed by a trusted source is one method employed to validate such code. Another option is to block all mobile code not from a trusted website.

NISTIR 8011 Vol. 3

A key alternate method for addressing mobile code is covered in NIST SP 800-53 control SC-44 (Detonation Chamber). Because SC-44 is not selected in the NIST SP 800-53B low, moderate, or high baselines, it is not included in this NISTIR. However, detonation chambers are effective in protecting against malicious mobile code, including mobile code downloaded from a web site, as well as mobile code in e-mails and attachments. Malicious mobile code is addressed further in the NISTIR 8011 volume on the boundary management capability.

Firmware is often considered to be a hybrid between hardware and software. For the purposes of this NISTIR, firmware is code stored in non-volatile memory that can be updated. The ability to update firmware allows hardware manufacturers great flexibility, reducing the need to replace hardware when issues are found or changes need to be made. Firmware that can be updated is subject to malicious code insertion, and thus needs protection under the SWAM capability. Generally, it is possible to compute a digital fingerprint for firmware. In addition, there are hardware mechanisms to validate firmware, such as the trusted platform module (TPM).

Code in memory is harder to protect than other forms of software addressed in this volume. Because changes to code in memory are very hard to detect, such changes can be very stealthy. However, the effects may be transient, lasting only until other code is loaded into memory. Since there are categories of in-memory attacks that do not disappear when other code is loaded into memory, assessment of controls related to code in memory are assigned to manual assessment.

2.4 Example SWAM Data Requirements[18]

Examples of data requirements for the SWAM *actual* state are provided in Table 3. Examples of data requirements for the SWAM *desired* state are provided in Table 4.

Table 3: Example SWAM Actual State Data Requirements

Data Item	Justification
The software installed on every device. To be usable for automated assessment, the data must be converted into a format that can be compared, by machine, with the authorized software inventory. Examples include: • Software Identification (SWID) tag;[a] and • Common Platform Enumeration (CPE). [b]	To identify when unauthorized software is installed on a device
Data necessary to determine how long unauthorized software has been present on a device. At a minimum: • Date/time unauthorized software was first discovered; and • Date/time unauthorized software was last seen.	To determine how long unauthorized software has been on a device.
Software blacklist[a] used to check device, to include version number or date of last update.[b]	• To determine if device was checked for unauthorized software. • To determine if the known-bad software blacklist is up-to-date per policy.

[a] Note that RFC 8412 provides a notification mechanism for reporting software installations as they occur using SWID tag data. https://www.rfc-editor.org/rfc/pdfrfc/rfc8412.txt.pdf.

[b] For more information on CPE, see https://csrc.nist.gov/projects/security-content-automation-protocol/specifications/cpe/.

[c] Blacklisted software is software that is not authorized to execute on a system; or prohibited Universal Resource Locators or websites.

[d] For blacklists, it is essential to keep the blacklist current, as new "known bad" software items are found. (This is one of the features of blacklisting that makes it less effective.) Whitelists only need to be updated on an event driven basis, e.g., when a version of software is replaced by a new version.

---

[18] Specific data required is variable based on organizational platforms, tools, configurations, etc.

Table 4: Example SWAM Desired State Data Requirements

Data Item	Justification
Authorized hardware inventory, to include assigned and authorized device attributes. See NISTIR 8011 Volume 2.	To identify what devices to check against what software defect checks.
The associated value for device attributes.[a]	To prioritize defects associated with devices.
Sets of attributes designated as mutually exclusive per the organization's policy.	For comparison with the set of assigned device attributes.
1. A listing of all authorized software for the organization to include data necessary to accurately identify the software product and compare to actual state data collected (vendor; product; version/release level/patch level; SWID tag; CPE; etc.). 2. Authoritative listing of executable software files associated with product. (With digital fingerprint of each file.) 3. Software Manager by device and product 4. Expiration policy. 5. Authorization status (dates initially authorized, last authorized, revoked, etc.)	• To calculate expiration dates for the authorization of software (1, 2, 4, 5). • To enable automated removal of differences that are not defects (all). • To be able to uniquely identify the software (1, 2). • To be able to validate that the software on the device is truly the software authorized (1, 2, 4, 5). • To know who to instruct to fix specific risk conditions found (3). • To assess each software manager's performance in risk management (all).
Management responsibility for each software management function for each authorized software product. Local enhancements[b] might include: • Approvers being assigned; • Managers being approved; and • Managers acknowledging receipt.	• To identify management responsibilities for ensuring that licensing, patching, and configuration standards are up-to-date. • To know who to instruct to fix specific risk conditions found. • To assess each such person's performance in risk management. *Note:* If not specified explicitly, management responsibility for each software management function is assumed to lie with the device manager.
A set of Software Profiles for the organization to include: • Associated attributes;[c] • Authorized software; • Mandatory software; • Organizationally prohibited software blacklist; • Industry blacklist;[d] and/or • Update frequency for blacklist.	• To compare with the software present on a device to determine defects. • To define authorized and unauthorized software on a per device basis. • To determine when software no longer authorized for the environment is being used for baselines. • To determine if known-bad blacklists are out of date.
Sets of device attributes that require a unique software profile when assigned to the same device, to include software profile(s) replaced and software profile(s) used.	To enforce more restrictive policies on devices that are assigned sets of attributes (e.g., database server and database authentication server).

[a] This value is defined by the organization, based on the value assigned by the organization to assets.
[b] Organizations can define additional data requirements and associated defects for the local environment.
[c] Software profiles have a one-to-many relationship with device attributes. One profile can have more than one device attribute associated with it (e.g., both Internal Web Server and External Web Server can map to the same Web Server software profile), but every device attribute is associated with exactly one software profile.
[d] Known bad blacklists are quite large, very dynamic, and often maintained by an antivirus or antimalware vendor. It is not expected that the organization knows what software is on the list, but that they know what blacklist is to be used and how frequently it is to be updated.

2.5 SWAM Concept of Operational Implementation

Figure 4: SWAM Concept of Operations (CONOPS) illustrates how SWAM might be implemented. The CONOPS is central to the automated assessment process.

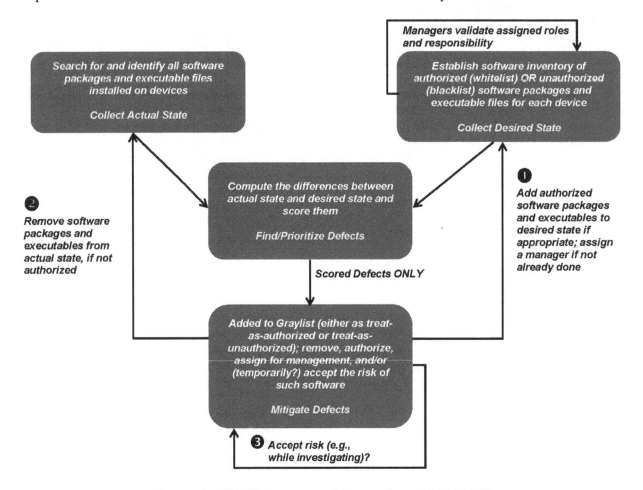

Figure 4: SWAM Concept of Operations (CONOPS)

The following is a brief description of the SWAM capability functionality:

> SWAM identifies software (including virtual machines) that is actually present on target network devices (the actual state) and compares it with the desired state inventory to determine if the identified software is authorized for operation and installation on target network devices.

2.5.1 Collect Actual State

Use tools to collect information about what software files and products are installed on target network devices, including files on mass storage, mobile code, firmware, and code in memory. Methods to detect (and possibly respond to) unauthorized software may include (but are not limited to):

- Identify software products through use of the operating system software database;

- Identify software files through the use of trusted digital fingerprint repositories;
- Link products to software files through a SWID tag;
- Whitelist authorized software and block all other software by default;
- Blacklist (and block by default) unauthorized and/or known malicious or unsafe software;
- Graylist (and block by default or allow by exception) until a determination is made of whether to authorize particular software;
- Require installation media to be digitally signed by a trusted source early in the supply chain to prevent tampering in the supply chain. Installation media can also include a signed SWID tag;
- Require all mobile code to be digitally signed by a trusted source; and
- Use a trusted platform module to verify the software used to boot the system.

Implementing some of the methods above to detect unauthorized software may require an agent on the host device to check new software (and software about to be executed) against associated policy constraints. A process to remove unauthorized software might also be implemented.

Unauthorized software may include any software not explicitly whitelisted or any software explicitly blacklisted. When unauthorized and/or malicious software is modified, even slightly, it is rendered invisible to blacklists, making blacklisting increasingly ineffective as malware variants become more easily produced. Because software whitelisting can block *any* unknown software, it is much more effective against unauthorized and/or malicious software.

The ISCM data collection process identifies the software files (and products) actually on the network and provides the information required to compare the software with the authorized inventory (desired state). Also, it is necessary to identify which devices in the target network are not reporting to discover the actual software operating on the devices.[19]

2.5.2 Collect Desired State

Create an authorized software inventory using policies, procedures, and processes suggested by the information security program or as otherwise defined by the organization. Expected output is an authorized software inventory that contains identifying information for software on a device—when it was authorized, when the authorization expires, and authorized digital signature. The digital signature may be contained in a SWID tag and/or in a separate trusted repository of known whitelisted/blacklisted software/signatures.

For maximum effectiveness, automated tools to manage software inventory using digital fingerprints include functionality to introduce new software into the trust repository. Such functionality allows the organization to include custom software unique to that organization, for

---

[19] Most monitoring software misses some devices on any given scan such as when mobile devices are off-network or when users turn devices off (e.g., while on vacation or official travel). The organization is expected to set standards for how many non-reporting devices to accept, and perhaps for how long (based on their practices and data collectors). The set standards are then measured by the data quality defect checks.

example. However, care is taken not to inadvertently whitelist malicious code as part of the software introduction process.

2.5.3 Find/Prioritize Defects

Comparing the list of software objects discovered on the network (actual state) with the authorized software inventory list (desired state) often reveals that software objects exist on one list but not on the other. The comparison identifies both unauthorized objects and missing authorized software that may indicate a security risk. Additional defects related to software asset management may be defined by the organization. Because of the high risk associated with unauthorized software installation, tools are available to block unauthorized software at first detection before the software is executed. Usually software blocking tools allow automatic blocking, or the user is asked whether to block or execute the software. In any case, after the comparison is complete, identified defects are scored and prioritized[20] (using federal- and organization-defined criteria) so that the appropriate response action can be taken (i.e., so that higher risk problems are addressed first).

2.6 SP 800-53 Control Items that Support SWAM

Section 2.6 describes how control items that support SWAM were identified as well as the nomenclature used to clarify each control item's focus on software.

2.6.1 Process for Identifying Needed Controls

In Volume 1 of NISTIR 8011, Section 3.5.2, Tracing Security Control Items to Capabilities, describes the process used to determine the controls needed to support a capability. In short, the two steps are:

1. Use an automated keyword search of the control text to identify control items that might support the capability. See keyword rules used for SWAM in Appendix B.

2. Manually identify those that *do* support the capability (true positives) and ignore those that do not (false positives).

Completion of the above two steps produces three sets of controls:

1. Control items in the low, moderate, and high baselines that support the SWAM capability (listed individually in Section 3.3 on SWAM Control (Item) Security Assessment Plan Narrative Tables and Templates, and listed by security baseline in Section 3.4 on Control Allocation Tables).

2. Control items in the low, moderate, and high baselines selected by the keyword search, but manually determined to be false positives (listed in Appendix C).

---

[20] A risk scoring methodology is necessary to score and prioritize defects but risk scoring is out of scope for this publication.

3. Control items not in a baseline, and not analyzed further after the keyword search, including:

   a. Program management (PM) controls, because PM controls do not apply to individual systems;

   b. Not selected controls—controls that are in SP 800-53 but are not assigned to (selected in) a baseline; and

   c. Privacy controls.

   The unanalyzed controls are listed in Appendix D, in case the organization wants to develop automated tests.

To implement whitelisting/blacklisting in general, and software whitelisting/blacklisting in particular, SWAM may rely on some other capabilities. The controls that support whitelisting and blacklisting are not included in SWAM if the supporting controls are more central to the other capability.

For example, configuration settings and/or user privilege lists are used to prevent anyone who is not a software manager from modifying the whitelists, graylists or blacklists. Moreover, the configuration settings and/or privileges are used to prevent the software managers from performing activities that could allow an outsider to misuse the software manager accounts to modify the desired state metadata. The same access controls are necessary to protect the actual state data. Assessment of such controls is left to the capabilities in which the control is central, rather than to the capability where applied (i.e., SWAM, in this case).

As a more specific example, controls supporting the PRIV capability are an important supplement to defect checks in all capabilities to ensure that only authorized persons can change the actual and desired state data, and the actual state of the system.

- For example, in SWAM, an attacker might try to change the trusted digital fingerprints of approved software files so that they may add or substitute malicious code. If the number of accounts authorized to make additions/substitutions is limited and only assigned to trusted persons with adequate separation of duties, such additions/substitutions are rendered more difficult.

- Also, if only a limited number of accounts are authorized to install software, it is harder for an attacker to find and exploit an account to inject malicious code.

Privileges to protect desired and actual state data are assessed in the PRIV capability, even though the privileges support SWAM and all other capabilities.

2.6.2 Control Item Nomenclature

Many control items that support the SWAM capability also support several other capabilities. For example, hardware, software products, software settings, and software patches may all benefit from configuration management controls. To clarify the scope of such control items as they relate to SWAM, expressions in the control item text are enclosed in curly brackets—for instance, {installed software}—to denote that a particular control item, as it supports the SWAM capability, focuses on, *and only on*, what is inside the curly brackets.

2.7 SWAM Specific Roles and Responsibilities

Table 5: Operational and Managerial Roles for SWAM, describes SWAM-specific roles and the corresponding responsibilities. Figure 5: Primary Roles in Automated Assessment of SWAM, shows how the roles integrate with the concept of operations. An organization implementing automated assessment can customize its approach by assigning (allocating) the responsibilities to persons in existing roles.

Table 5: Operational and Managerial Roles for SWAM

Role Code	Role Title	Role Description	Role Type
DM	Device Manager (DM)	Assigned to a specific device or group of devices, device managers are (for HWAM) responsible for adding/removing devices from the network, and for configuring the hardware of each device (adding and removing hardware components). The device managers are specified in the desired state inventory specification. The device manager may be a person or a group. If a group, there is a group manager in charge. In the absence of a Software Manager (SWMan), the DM may be assigned the task of removing unauthorized software.	Operational
Auth	Authorizers	Authorizers have the responsibility of authorizing specific items (e.g., devices, software, software installers, software locations, or settings), and thereby define the desired state. In special cases they authorize people to authorize other items. The desired state manager oversees and organizes the activity of authorization.	Operational
DSM	Desired State Managers (DSM)	Desired State Managers are needed for both the ISCM Target Network and each assessment object. The desired state managers ensure that data specifying the desired state of the relevant capability is entered into the ISCM system's desired state data and is available to guide the actual state collection subsystem and to identify defects. The DSM for the ISCM Target Network also resolves any ambiguity about which system authorization boundary has defects (if any). Authorizers share some of the responsibilities by authorizing specific items (e.g., devices, software, or settings), and thus defining the desired state, as delegated by the DSM. The DSM oversees and organizes this activity.	Operational
ISCM-Ops	ISCM Operators (ISCM-Ops)	ISCM operators are responsible for operating the ISCM system (see ISCM-Sys).	Operational

Role Code	Role Title	Role Description	Role Type
ISCM-Sys	The system that collects, analyzes and displays ISCM security-related information	The ISCM system: a) collects the desired state specification; b) collects security-related information from sensors (e.g., scanners, agents, training applications, etc.); and c) processes that information into a useful form. To support task c) the system conducts specified defect check(s) and sends defect information to an ISCM dashboard covering the relevant system(s). The ISCM system is responsible for the assessment of most SP 800-53 security controls.	Operational
MAN	Manual Assessors	Assessments not automated by the ISCM system are conducted by human assessors using manual/procedural methods. Manual/procedural assessments might also be conducted to verify the automated security-related information collected by the ISCM system—when there is a concern about data quality.	Operational
RskEx	Risk Executive, System Owner, and/or Authorizing Official (RskEx)	Defined in SPs 800-37 and 800-39.[21]	Managerial
SWMan	Software Manager	Assigned to specific devices and responsible for installing and/or removing software from the device. The key aspects of the Software Manager responsibility are to ONLY install authorized software and to promptly remove ALL unauthorized software found. The software manager is also responsible for ensuring software media is available to support roll back of changes and restoration of software to prior states. This role might be performed by the DM (Device Manager) and/or the PatMan (Patch Manager). If users are authorized to install software, they are also SWMans (Software Managers) for the relevant devices.	Operational
TBD	To be determined by the organization	Depends on specific use. TBD by the organization.	Unknown

---

[21] Joint Task Force Transformation Initiative, Risk Management Framework for Information Systems and Organizations, (2018), (National Institute of Standards and Technology, Gaithersburg, MD), NIST Special Publication (SP) 800-37, https://csrc.nist.gov/publications/detail/sp/800-37/rev-2/final;
Joint Task Force Transformation Initiative, Managing Information Security Risk: Organization, Mission, and Information System View (2011), (National Institute of Standards and Technology, Gaithersburg, MD), NIST Special Publication (SP) 800-39, https://doi.org/10.6028/NIST.SP.800-39.

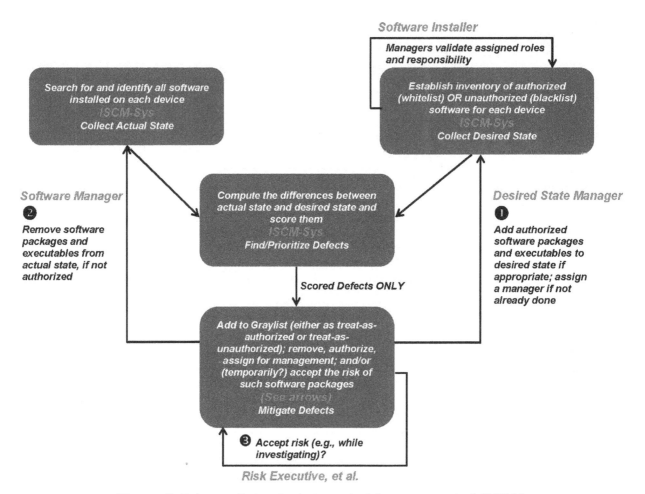

Figure 5: Primary Roles in Automated Assessment of SWAM

2.8 SWAM Assessment Boundary

The assessment boundary is ideally all software on an entire *network* of computers from the innermost enclave out to where the network either ends in an air-gap or interconnects to other network(s)—typically the Internet or the network(s) of a partner or partners. For SWAM, the boundary includes software on all devices inside the assessment boundary and associated components, including software on removable devices found at the time of the scan. For more detail and definitions of some of the terms applicable to the assessment boundary, see Section 4.3.2 in Volume 1 of this NISTIR.

2.9 SWAM Actual State and Desired State Specification

For information on the actual state and the desired state specification for SWAM, see the assessment criteria notes section of the defect check tables in Section 3.2.

Note that many controls in SWAM refer to developing and updating an inventory of software on devices (or other inventories). Note also, that per the SP 800-53A[22] definition of *test*, testing of the SWAM controls implies the need for specification of both an actual state inventory and a desired state inventory, so that the test can compare the two inventories. The details of the comparison are described in the defect check tables in Section 3.2.

2.10 SWAM Authorization Boundary and Inheritance

See Section 4.3.1 of Volume 1 of this NISTIR for information on how authorization boundaries are addressed in automated assessment. In short, for SWAM, software on each device is assigned to one and only one authorization (system) boundary, per SP 800-53 CM-08(5), entitled "Information System Component Inventory | No Duplicate Accounting of Components." The ISCM dashboard can include a mechanism for recording the assignment of software to authorization boundaries, making sure all software are assigned to at least one authorization boundary, and that no software product is assigned to more than one authorization boundary.

For information on how inheritance of common controls is managed, see Section 4.3.3 of Volume 1 of this NISTIR. For SWAM, many utilities, database management software products, web server software objects, and parts of the operating system provide inheritable support and/or controls for other systems. The ISCM dashboard can include a mechanism to record information about inheritance and use it in assessing the system's overall risk.

2.11 SWAM Assessment Criteria Recommended Scores and Risk-Acceptance Thresholds

General guidance on options for risk scores[23] to be used to set thresholds is outside the scope of this NISTIR and is being developed elsewhere. In any case, for SWAM, organizations are encouraged to use metrics that look at both average risk score and maximum risk score per device.

2.12 SWAM Assessment Criteria Device Groupings to Consider

To support automated assessment and ongoing authorization, software is clearly grouped by authorization boundary [see Control Items CM-8a and CM-8(5) in SP 800-53] and by the software managers responsible for software installation on specific devices[24] [see Control Item CM-8(4) in SP 800-53]. In addition to these two important groupings, the organization may want to use other groupings for risk analysis, as discussed in Section 5.6 of Volume 1 of this NISTIR.

---

[22] Joint Task Force Transformation Initiative (2014), Assessing Security and Privacy Controls in Federal Information Systems and Organizations (National Institute of Standards and Technology, Gaithersburg, MD), NIST Special Publication (SP) 800-53A, https://doi.org/10.6028/NIST.SP.800-53Ar4.
[23] A risk score, also called a *defect score*, in the context of SWAM, is a measure of how exploitable a defect is.
[24] The Software Manager (SWMan) role is responsible for installing on and removing software from the device, but the role might be performed by the device manager or other responsible party in a specific organization.

3. SWAM Security Assessment Plan Documentation Template

3.1 Introduction and Steps for Adapting This Plan

This section provides templates for the security assessment plan in accordance with SP 800-37 and SP 800-53A. The documentation elements are described in Section 6 of Volume 1 of this NISTIR. Section 9 of the same volume specifically describes how the templates and documentation relate to the assessment tasks and work products defined in SP 800-37 and SP 800-53A. The following are suggested steps to adapt this plan to the organization's needs and implement automated monitoring.

Figure 6 shows the main steps in the adaptation process. The steps are expanded to more detail in the following three sections.

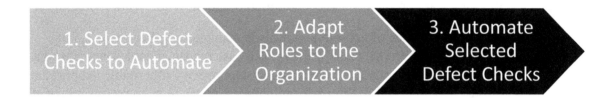

Figure 6: Main Steps in Adapting the Plan Template

3.1.1 Select Defect Checks to Automate

The main steps in selecting defect checks to automate are described in this section.

Figure 7: Sub-Steps to Select Defect Checks to Automate

Take the following steps to select which defect checks to automate:

(1) **Identify Assessment Boundary:** Identify the assessment boundary to be covered. (See Section 4.3 of Volume 1 of this NISTIR.)

(2) **Identify System Impact:** Identify the Federal Information Processing Standard (FIPS) 199 impact level (high water mark) for the assessment boundary.[25] Also see SP 800-60 and/or organizational categorization records.[26]

(3) **Review Security Assessment Plan Documentation:**

    a. Review the defect checks documented in Section 3.2 to get an initial sense of the proposed items to be tested.

    b. Review the security assessment plan narratives in Section 3.2 to understand how the defect checks apply to the controls that support Software Asset Management.

(4) **Select Defect Checks:**

    a. Based on Steps (1) to (3) in this list and an understanding of the organization's risk tolerance, use Table 6: Mapping of Attack Steps to Security Sub-Capability, in Section 3.2.3 to identify the defect checks necessary to test the effectiveness of controls based on the impact level and risk tolerance.

    b. Mark the defect checks necessary as selected in Section 3.2.2. The organization is not required to use automation, but automation of testing adds value to the extent that it:

        (i) Produces assessment results accurately, completely, and timely enough to better defend against attacks; and/or

        (ii) Reduces the cost of assessment over the long term.

3.1.2 Adapt Roles to the Organization

The main steps to adapt the roles to the organization are described in this section.

Figure 8: Sub-Steps to Adapt Roles to the Organization

(1) **Review Proposed Roles**: Proposed roles are described in Section 2.7, SWAM Specific Roles and Responsibilities (Illustrative).

(2) **Address Missing Roles:** Identify any required roles not currently assigned in the organization. Determine how to assign the unassigned roles.

(3) **Rename Roles:** Identify the organization-specific names that match each role. (Note that more than one proposed role might be performed by the same organizational role.)

---

[25] National Institute of Standards and Technology (2004), Standards for Security Categorization of Federal Information and Information Systems, Federal Information Processing Standard (FIPS) 199, https://doi.org/10.6028/NIST.FIPS.199.

[26] Stine K et al (2008), Guide for Mapping Types of Information and Information Systems to Security Categories (National Institute of Standards and Technology, Gaithersburg, MD), NIST Special Publication (SP) 800-60, https://doi.org/10.6028/NIST.SP.800-60v1r1.

(4) **Adjust Documentation:** Map the organization-specific roles to the roles proposed herein, in one of two ways (either may be acceptable):

    a. Add a column to the table in Section 2.7 for the organization-specific role and list it there; or

    b. Use global replace to change the role names throughout the documentation from the names proposed here to the organization-specific names.

3.1.3 Automate Selected Defect Checks

The main steps to implement automation are described in this section.

Figure 9: Sub-Steps to Automate Selected Defect Checks

(1) **Add Defect Checks:** Review the defect check definition and add checks as needed based on organizational risk tolerance and expected attack types. [Role: DSM (See Section 2.7.)]

(2) **Adjust Data Collection:**

    a. Review the actual state information needed and configure automated sensors to collect the required information. [Role: ISCM-Sys (See Section 2.7)]

    b. Review the matching desired state specification that was specified or add additional specifications to match the added actual state to be checked. Configure the collection system to receive and store this desired state specification in a form that can be automatically compared to the actual state data. [Role: ISCM-Sys (See Section 2.7.)]

(3) **Operate the ISCM-System:**

    a. Operate the collection system to identify both security and data quality defects.

    b. Configure the collection system to send security and data quality information to the defect management dashboard.

(4) **Use the Results to Manage Risk:** Use the results to respond to higher risk findings first and to measure potential residual risk to inform aggregate risk acceptance decisions. If risk is determined to be too great for acceptance, the results may also be used to help prioritize mitigation actions or as rationale for denial of continued authorization to operate.

3.2 SWAM Sub-Capabilities and Defect Check Tables and Templates

This section documents the specific test templates that are proposed and considered adequate to assess the control items that support Software Asset Management. See Section 5 of Volume 1 of this NISTIR for an overview of defect checks and see Section 4.1 of Volume 1 for an overview of the actual state and desired state specifications discussed in the Assessment Criteria Notes for each defect check. Sections 3.2.1, 3.2.2, and 3.2.3 of this document describe the foundational, data quality, and local defect checks, respectively. The *Supporting Control Item(s)* data in sections 3.2.1, 3.2.2, and 3.2.3 specify which controls, when ineffective, might cause a particular defect check to fail. The association between control items and defect checks provides further documentation on why the check (test) might be needed. Refer to Section 3.1 for how to adapt the defect checks (and roles specified therein) to the organization.

Data found in this section can be used in both defect check selection and root cause analysis. Section 3.2.4 documents how each sub-capability (tested by a defect check) serves to support the overall capability by addressing certain example attack steps and/or data quality issues. Appendix G can also be used to support root cause analysis. The Defect Check Templates are organized as follows:

- In the section beginning "*The purpose of this sub-capability…*," the sub-capability being tested by the defect check is defined and assessment criteria described. How the sub-capabilities block or delay certain example attack steps is described in Section 3.2.4.

- In the section beginning "*The defect check to assess…*," the defect check name and the assessment criteria to be used to assess whether the sub-capability is effective in achieving its purpose are described.

- In the section beginning "*Example Responses*," examples of potential responses when the check finds a defect, and what role is likely responsible are described. Potential responses (with example primary responsibility assignments) are common actions and are appropriate when defects are discovered in a given sub-capability. The example primary responsibility assignments do not change the overall management responsibilities defined in other NIST guidance. Moreover, the response actions and responsibilities can be customized by each organization to best adapt to local circumstances.

- Finally, in the section beginning "*Supporting Control Items,*" the control items that work together to support the sub-capability are listed. Identification of the supporting control items is based on the mapping of defect checks to control items in Section 3.3. Each sub-capability is supported by a set of control items. Thus, if any of the listed supporting controls fail, the defect check fails and overall risk is likely to increase.

As noted in Section 3.1, this material is designed to be customized and adapted to become part of an organization's security assessment plan.

3.2.1 Foundational Sub-Capabilities and Corresponding Defect Checks

NISTIR 8011 Volume 3 proposes four foundational security-oriented defect checks for the SWAM capability. The foundational checks are designated SWAM-F01 through SWAM-F04.

The foundational defect checks were selected for their value for summary reporting. The *Selected* column indicates which of the checks are implemented by the organization. Defect checks may be computed for individual checks (e.g., foundational, data quality, or local), or summarized for various groupings of devices (e.g., device manager, device owner, system, etc.) out to the full assessment boundary.

Note for SWAM: SWAM defect checks F01, F02 and F03 provide alternate ways to detect the blocking or limiting of execution of unauthorized software from a mass storage device. Organizations select one or more of the defect check(s) F01, F02, and/or F03 based on organizational assurance needs and organization-specific control implementations. Organizations may determine that risk is sufficiently mitigated by applying defect check F01 only in specified locations associated with F03 and/or as installed by authorized installers associated with F02; however, SWAM defect check F04 is needed separately to detect malicious code in memory.

3.2.1.1 Prevent Unauthorized Software from Executing *Sub-Capability and Defect Check SWAM-F01*

The purpose of this sub-capability is defined as follows:

Sub-Capability Name	Sub-Capability Purpose	Selected
Prevent unauthorized software from executing	Prevent or reduce the execution of unauthorized software (presumed malware).	Yes

The defect check to assess whether this sub-capability is operating effectively is defined as follows:

Defect Check ID	Defect Check Name	Assessment Criteria Notes
SWAM-F01	Unauthorized software executes	1) The actual state is the list (inventory) of all software files that the system has loaded (or attempted to load) for execution, identified by digital fingerprints or equivalents, e.g., digitally signed files or libraries. 2) The desired state specification is a list of all software files authorized to be executed, identified by digital fingerprints or equivalents. 3) A defect is a software file that is executed (or attempted to be executed) that is not on the list of files authorized to be executed. *Note:* F01 addresses distribution supply chain issues if the organization gets software file message digests (encrypted and signed) from the software developer or other equally trusted source.

Example Responses:

Defect Check ID	Potential Response Action	Primary Responsibility
SWAM-F01	Automatically block execution on detection	ISCM-Ops
SWAM-F01	Remove the software	SWMan
SWAM-F01	Authorize the software	Auth
SWAM-F01	Accept risk	RskEx
SWAM-F01	Oversee and coordinate response	DSM

FOUNDATIONAL DEFECT CHECKS

Supporting Control Items:

Defect Check ID	Baseline	SP 800-53 Control Item Code
SWAM-F01	Low	CM-7(b)
SWAM-F01	Low	CM-11(b)
SWAM-F01	Low	SI-3(b)
SWAM-F01	Low	SI-3(c)
SWAM-F01	Moderate	CM-7(1)(b)
SWAM-F01	Moderate	CM-7(2)
SWAM-F01	Moderate	CM-7(4)(a)
SWAM-F01	Moderate	CM-7(4)(b)
SWAM-F01	Moderate	MA-3(2)
SWAM-F01	Moderate	SC-18(a)
SWAM-F01	Moderate	SC-18(b)
SWAM-F01	Moderate	SC-18(c)
SWAM-F01	Moderate	SI-7
SWAM-F01	High	CM-5(3)
SWAM-F01	High	CM-7(5)(a)
SWAM-F01	High	CM-7(5)(b)
SWAM-F01	High	SA-12

3.2.1.2 Prevent or Reduce Execution of Software from Unauthorized Installers *Sub-Capability and Defect Check SWAM-F02*

The purpose of this sub-capability is defined as follows:

Sub-Capability Name	Sub-Capability Purpose
Prevent or reduce execution of software from unauthorized installers	Prevent or reduce the execution of software (presumed malware) installed by an unauthorized installer.

The defect check to assess whether this sub-capability is operating effectively is defined as follows:

Defect Check ID	Defect Check Name	Assessment Criteria Notes	Selected
SWAM-F02	Unauthorized software installer	1) The actual state is the list (inventory) of all software that is being executed or has been loaded for execution over a specified period of time defined by the organization. 2) The desired state specification is a list of all software installed by an authorized installer account. 3) A defect is software that is executed (or attempted to execute) that was not installed by an authorized installer account. *Note:* An alternate version of this defect check could operate on all installed software, rather than executing software. The check could operate on both for defense in depth purposes.	Yes

Example Responses:

Defect Check ID	Potential Response Action	Primary Responsibility
SWAM-F02	Automatically block installation by unauthorized persons	ISCM-Ops
SWAM-F02	Automatically block execution on detection	ISCM-Ops
SWAM-F02	Remove the software	SWMan
SWAM-F02	Authorize the software/installer	Auth
SWAM-F02	Accept risk	RskEx
SWAM-F02	Oversee and coordinate response	DSM

FOUNDATIONAL DEFECT CHECKS

Supporting Control Items:

Defect Check ID	Baseline	SP 800-53 Control Item Code
SWAM-F02	Low	CM-11(a)
SWAM-F02	Low	CM-11(b)
SWAM-F02	Moderate	CM-7(1)(b)
SWAM-F02	Moderate	CM-7(2)
SWAM-F02	Moderate	CM-7(4)(a)
SWAM-F02	Moderate	CM-7(4)(b)
SWAM-F02	Moderate	SI-3(1)
SWAM-F02	High	CM-7(5)(a)
SWAM-F02	High	CM-7(5)(b)

3.2.1.3 Prevent or Reduce Software Execution from Unauthorized Location *Sub-Capability and Defect Check SWAM-F03*

The purpose of this sub-capability is defined as follows:

Sub-Capability Name	Sub-Capability Purpose
Prevent or reduce software execution from unauthorized location	Prevent or reduce the execution of software (presumed malware) loaded from an uncontrolled or unauthorized location.

The defect check to assess whether this sub-capability is operating effectively is defined as follows:

Defect Check ID	Defect Check Name	Assessment Criteria Notes	Selected
SWAM-F03	Unauthorized software directory/folder location	1) The actual state is the list (inventory) of all software files (identified by the location from which loaded, or equivalent) that are being executed or have been loaded for execution over a period of time defined by the organization. (The actual value to be stored in the inventory is a tuple consisting of the file and the location from which loaded.) 2) The desired state specification is a list of all software files that exist in the authorized location. (The actual value to be stored in the specification is one tuple for each authorized file and a location from which it is permitted to be loaded.) 3) A defect is a software file that is executed (or attempted to be executed) that is not loaded from an authorized location. (The actual state tuple does not match a desired state tuple.) *Note:* Authorized locations are to be restricted via access controls to be writable only by authorized installer accounts.	Yes

Example Responses:

Defect Check ID	Potential Response Action	Primary Responsibility
SWAM-F03	Automatically block execution on detection of wrong location	ISCM-Ops
SWAM-F03	Remove the software	SWMan
SWAM-F03	Authorize the software/location for execution	Auth
SWAM-F03	Accept risk	RskEx
SWAM-F03	Oversee and coordinate response	DSM

FOUNDATIONAL DEFECT CHECKS

Supporting Control Items:

Defect Check ID	Baseline	SP 800-53 Control Item Code
SWAM-F03	Low	CM-7(b)
SWAM-F03	Low	CM-11(b)
SWAM-F03	Moderate	CM-7(1)(b)
SWAM-F03	Moderate	CM-7(2)
SWAM-F03	Moderate	CM-7(4)(a)
SWAM-F03	Moderate	CM-7(4)(b)
SWAM-F03	High	CM-7(5)(a)
SWAM-F03	High	CM-7(5)(b)

3.2.1.4 Ensure or Increase Trust of System Software at Startup *Sub-Capability and Defect Check SWAM-F04*

The purpose of this sub-capability is defined as follows:

Sub-Capability Name	Sub-Capability Purpose	Selected
Ensure or increase trust of system software at startup	Prevent or reduce the insertion of malware into key system components before or during system startup.	Yes

The defect check to assess whether this sub-capability is operating effectively is defined as follows:

Defect Check ID	Defect Check Name	Assessment Criteria Notes
SWAM-F04	Untrusted core software	1) The actual state is data on the integrity of organizationally selected software components observed at startup. At a minimum, core components are expected to include root operating system elements, firmware, etc. Digital fingerprints are often used to identify components in the actual state. 2) The desired state specification is a list of the approved version of each software element using the same methods of identification (digital fingerprint, digital signature, etc.). 3) A defect is software observed at startup that was not in the desired state specification.

Example Responses:

Defect Check ID	Potential Response Action	Primary Responsibility
SWAM-F04	Lock the system and block use	ISCM-Ops
SWAM-F04	Restore authorized state/software	SWMan
SWAM-F04	Authorize the new state	Auth
SWAM-F04	Accept risk	RskEx
SWAM-F04	Oversee and coordinate response	DSM

FOUNDATIONAL DEFECT CHECKS

Supporting Control Items:

Defect Check ID	Baseline	SP 800-53 Control Item Code
SWAM-F04	Low	CM-11(b)
SWAM-F04	Low	SI-3(b)
SWAM-F04	Moderate	CM-7(1)(b)
SWAM-F04	Moderate	CM-7(4)(a)
SWAM-F04	Moderate	CM-7(4)(b)
SWAM-F04	Moderate	SI-7(1)
SWAM-F04	High	CM-5(3)
SWAM-F04	High	CM-7(5)(a)
SWAM-F04	High	CM-7(5)(b)

3.2.2 Data Quality Sub-Capabilities and Corresponding Defect Checks

NISTIR 8011 Volume 3 proposes four *data quality* defect checks, designated SWAM-Q01 through SWAM-Q04. The data quality defect checks are important because they provide the information necessary to determine how reliable the overall assessment automation process is, information which can be used to decide how much to trust the other defect check data (i.e., provide greater assurance about security control effectiveness). The data quality defect checks were selected for their value for summary reporting and are not associated with specific control items. The *Selected* column indicates which of the checks is implemented by the organization. Data quality checks are described more completely in NISTIR 8011, Volume 1, Overview, Section 5.5. Data Quality Measures.

3.2.2.1 Ensure Completeness of Device-Level Reporting *Sub-Capability and Defect Check SWAM-Q01*

The purpose of this sub-capability is defined as follows:

Sub-Capability Name	Sub-Capability Purpose
Ensure completeness of device-level reporting	Ensure that devices are correctly reporting SWAM related information to the actual state inventory to prevent SWAM defects from going undetected.

The defect check to assess whether this sub-capability is operating effectively is defined as follows:

Defect Check ID	Defect Check Name	Assessment Criteria Notes	Selected
SWAM-Q01	Non-reporting of device-level SWAM information	1) The actual state is the list of devices connected to the assessment boundary. 2) The desired state is that all the devices in the actual state are reporting SWAM information. 3) A defect occurs when a device in the actual state has not reported its SWAM information as recently as expected. Criteria developed to define the threshold for "as recently as expected," for each device or device type are based on the following considerations: a. some devices (e. g., domain controllers, routers) must always be present. b. endpoints may not report in a particular collection because they are turned off, network connections are temporarily down, etc. But the endpoints should appear in the actual state at least every n collections, where "n" is defined by "as recently as expected." c. defining "as recently as expected" for devices such as laptops might require information on what percent of the time the devices are expected to be connected to the network and powered on. As that percent goes down, the length of "as recently as expected" goes up. Time and experience are required to accurately define "as recently as expected" for each device/device type in order to eliminate false positives while still finding true positives.	Yes

DATA QUALITY DEFECT CHECKS

Example Responses:

Defect Check ID	Potential Response Action	Primary Responsibility
SWAM-Q01	Restore device reporting of software	ISCM-Ops
SWAM-Q01	Declare device missing (with software)	DM
SWAM-Q01	Accept risk	RskEx
SWAM-Q01	Oversee and coordinate response	ISCM-Ops

Supporting Control Items:

Defect Check ID	Baseline	SP 800-53 Control Item Code
SWAM-Q01	Low	CM-8(a)

3.2.2.2 Ensure Completeness of Defect-Check-Level Reporting *Sub-Capability and Defect Check SWAM-Q02*

The purpose of this sub-capability is defined as follows:

Sub-Capability Name	Sub-Capability Purpose	Selected
Ensure completeness of defect-check-level reporting	Ensure that defect check information is correctly reported in the actual state inventory to prevent systematic inability to check any defect on any device.	Yes

The defect check to assess whether this sub-capability is operating effectively is defined as follows:

Defect Check ID	Defect Check Name	Assessment Criteria Notes
SWAM-Q02	Non-reporting of defect checks	1) The actual state is the set of SWAM data that was collected in each collection cycle to support all implemented SWAM defect checks. 2) The desired state is the set of SWAM data that must be collected in each collection cycle to support all implemented SWAM defect checks. 3) The defect is any set of data needed for a defect check where not all the data was collected for an organizationally specified number of devices, indicating that the collection system is not providing enough information to perform a sufficiently thorough assessment.

Example Responses:

Defect Check ID	Potential Response Action	Primary Responsibility
SWAM-Q02	Restore defect check reporting	ISCM-Ops
SWAM-Q02	Accept risk	RskEx
SWAM-Q02	Oversee and coordinate response	ISCM-Ops

Supporting Control Items:

Defect Check ID	Baseline	SP 800-53 Control Item Code
SWAM-Q02	Low	CM-8(a)

3.2.2.3 Increase Overall Reporting Completeness *Sub-Capability and Defect Check SWAM-Q03*

The purpose of this sub-capability is defined as follows:

Sub-Capability Name	Sub-Capability Purpose
Increase overall reporting completeness	Ensure that data for as many defect checks as possible are correctly reported in the actual state inventory to prevent defects from persisting undetected across the assessment boundary.

The defect check to assess whether this sub-capability is operating effectively is defined as follows:

Defect Check ID	Defect Check Name	Assessment Criteria Notes	Selected
SWAM-Q03	Low completeness-metric	The completeness metric is not a device-level defect but is applied to any collection of devices – for example, those in a system authorization boundary. The completeness metric is used in assessing the accuracy of the collection system. 1) The actual state is the number of specified defect checks provided by the collection system in a reporting window. 2) The desired state is the number of specified defect checks that should have been provided in that same reporting window. 3) Completeness is the metric defined as the actual state number divided by the desired state number – that is, the completeness metric is the percentage of specified defect checks collected during the reporting window. Completeness measures long term ability to collect all needed data. 4) A defect is when completeness is too low (based on the defined threshold). This indicates risk because, when completeness is too low, there is a higher risk of defects being undetected. An acceptable level of completeness balances technical feasibility against the need for 100% completeness. *Note on 1):* A specific check-device combination may only be counted once in the required minimal reporting period. For example, if checks are to be done every 3 days, a check done twice in that timeframe would still count as 1 check. However, if there are 30 days in the reporting window, that check-device combination could be counted for each of the ten 3-day periods included. *Note on 2):* For example, suppose that there are 4 devices and the organization requires that 20 SWAM-specific defect checks be performed on each device, for a total of 80. If only 3 devices are checked but all 20 defects are checked on those 3 devices, then 60 out of 80 is the completeness metric. If all four devices are checked and the number of defect checks performed on each device is 5, 10, 15, and 20, then 50 out of 80 is the completeness metric for the SWAM-specific defect checks.	Yes

Example Responses:

Defect Check ID	Potential Response Action	Primary Responsibility
SWAM-Q03	Restore completeness	ISCM-Ops
SWAM-Q03	Accept risk	RskEx
SWAM-Q03	Oversee and coordinate response	ISCM-Ops

Supporting Control Items:

Defect Check ID	Baseline	SP 800-53 Control Item Code
SWAM-Q03	Low	CM-8(a)

3.2.2.4 Ensure Overall Reporting Timeliness *Sub-Capability and Defect Check SWAM-Q04*

The purpose of this sub-capability is defined as follows:

Sub-Capability Name	Sub-Capability Purpose
Ensure overall reporting timeliness	Ensure that data for as many defect checks as possible are reported in a timely manner in the actual state inventory to prevent defects from persisting undetected. To be effective, defects need to be found and mitigated considerably faster than they can be exploited.

The defect check to assess whether this sub-capability is operating effectively is defined as follows:

Defect Check ID	Defect Check Name	Assessment Criteria Notes	Selected
SWAM-Q04	Poor timeliness metric	The Timeliness metric is not a device-level defect, but can be applied to any collection of devices – for example, those within a system (authorization boundary). It is used in computing the maturity of the collection system. 1) The actual state is the number of specified defect checks provided by the collection system in one collection cycle – the period in which each defect should be checked once. 2) The desired state is the number of specified defect checks that should have been provided in the collection cycle. 3) Timeliness is the metric defined as the actual state number divided by the desired state number – that is, it is the percentage of specified defect checks collected in the reporting cycle. Thus it measures the percentage of data that is currently timely (collected as recently as required). 4) A defect is when "timeliness" is too poor (based on the defined threshold). This indicates risk because when timeliness is poor there is a higher risk of defects not being detected quickly enough. *Note on 1):* A specific check-device combination may only be counted once in the collection cycle. *Note on 2):* Different devices may have different sets of specified checks, based on their role.	Yes

Example Responses:

Defect Check ID	Potential Response Action	Primary Responsibility
SWAM-Q04	Restore frequency	ISCM-Ops
SWAM-Q04	Accept risk	RskEx
SWAM-Q04	Oversee and coordinate response	ISCM-Ops

Supporting Control Items:

Defect Check ID	Baseline	SP 800-53 Control Item Code
SWAM-Q04	Low	CM-8(b)
SWAM-Q04	Low	CM-11(c)
SWAM-Q04	Moderate	CM-8(1)

3.2.3 Local Sub-Capabilities and Corresponding Defect Checks

This section includes local defect checks, as examples of what organizations may add to the foundational and data quality checks to provide more complete automated assessment of SP 800-53 controls that support SWAM.

Organizations exercise authority to manage risk by choosing whether to select specific defect checks for implementation. In general, selecting more defect checks may lower risk (if there is capacity to address defects found) and provide greater assurance but may also increase cost of detection and mitigation. The organization selects defect checks for implementation (or not) to balance the benefits and costs and prioritize risk response actions by focusing first on the problems that pose greater risk (i.e., managing risk).

Note that each local defect check may also include options to make the defect check more or less rigorous, as the risk tolerance of the organization and impact level of the system indicates.

The "Selected" column is present to indicate which of the local defect checks the organization chooses to implement as documented or as modified by the organization.

3.2.3.1 Ensure or Increase Integrity of Software Authorizers *Sub-Capability and Defect Check SWAM-L01*

The purpose of this sub-capability is defined as follows:

Sub-Capability Name	Sub-Capability Purpose
Ensure or increase integrity of software authorizers	Prevent or reduce the insertion of malware into the list of approved software by unauthorized persons.

The defect check to assess whether this sub-capability is operating effectively is defined as follows:

Defect Check ID	Defect Check Name	Assessment Criteria Notes	Selected
SWAM-L01	Unapproved authorizer	1) The actual state is the account which authorized the use of each instance of software. 2) The desired state specification is a list of the approved accounts which can authorize software 3) A defect is software that was authorized by an unapproved authorizer. *Note on 1): An instance of software* authorized for use is specified at the level of granularity the organization deems appropriate, based on the organization's business needs and risk tolerance. An *instance* is likely a software *product*, but might be a software *file*, an *Internet domain*, or a *URL*. Instances of software might be authorized for all devices, specific types of devices, or specific individual devices.	TBD by organization

Example Responses:

Defect Check ID	Potential Response Action	Primary Responsibility
SWAM-L01	Block the software as unauthorized	ISCM-Ops
SWAM-L01	Remove the software	SWMan
SWAM-L01	Authorized person approves the software	Auth
SWAM-L01	Accept risk	RskEx
SWAM-L01	Oversee and coordinate response	DSM

Supporting Control Items:

Defect Check ID	Baseline	SP 800-53 Control Item Code
SWAM-L01	Low	CM-4
SWAM-L01	Moderate	SI-7
SWAM-L01	High	SI-7(14)(b)

3.2.3.2 Prevent or Reduce (Careless or Malicious) Software Approval *Sub-Capability and Defect Check SWAM-L02*

The purpose of this sub-capability is defined as follows:

Sub-Capability Name	Sub-Capability Purpose
Prevent or reduce (careless or malicious) software approval	Ensure checks and balances are in place to prevent a single individual from carelessly or maliciously changing authorization of software installation. *Note 1:* If the organization chooses to use access restrictions to enforce multiple approvals, effectiveness is assessed under the PRIV capability. *Note 2:* See SWAM-L09 for authorization boundary.

The defect check to assess whether this sub-capability is operating effectively is defined as follows:

Defect Check ID	Defect Check Name	Assessment Criteria Notes	Selected
SWAM-L02	Required authorizations missing	1) The actual state is the list of persons who authorized the change to the system, thus allowing the software item to be executed. This would typically be recorded in the desired state inventory as part of the configuration change control process. 2) The desired state is the list of persons who are authorized to approve system changes and allow software to be executed. This may include specifying first, second, etc., approver roles. 3) A defect occurs when the software item is authorized a. by fewer than the required number of distinct and authorized approvers; or b. by persons not authorized to approve software. *Note:* An organization may wish to enhance this defect check by requiring different individuals to verify different attributes of the software, such as supply chain strength, vendors' attention to security, etc.	TBD by organization

Example Responses:

Defect Check ID	Potential Response Action	Primary Responsibility
SWAM-L02	Block the software as unauthorized	ISCM-Ops
SWAM-L02	Remove the software	SWMan
SWAM-L02	Authorized person approves the software	Auth
SWAM-L02	Accept risk	RskEx
SWAM-L02	Oversee and coordinate response	DSM

Supporting Control Items:

Defect Check ID	Baseline	SP 800-53 Control Item Code
SWAM-L02	Low	CM-4
SWAM-L02	Moderate	SI-7

3.2.3.3 Promptly Determine and Address Needed Installation and Deinstallation of Software *Sub-Capability and Defect Check SWAM-L03*

The purpose of this sub-capability is defined as follows:

Sub-Capability Name	Sub-Capability Purpose
Promptly determine and address needed installation and deinstallation of software	Ensure that needed changes are addressed in a timely manner by flagging requested changes not considered (approved and implemented; or disapproved) in a timely manner as risks.

The defect check to assess whether this sub-capability is operating effectively is defined as follows:

Defect Check ID	Defect Check Name	Assessment Criteria Notes	Selected
SWAM-L03	Expired actions on software authorization/deauthorization requests	1) The actual state includes: a. a list of proposed changes to the desired state. b. a list of approved changes to the actual state, likely derived from the desired state specification. c. the date the change was proposed. d. the date the change was implemented (if approved) or the date the change was rejected. 2) The desired state includes: a. the timeframe within which proposed items are to be approved or rejected. b. the timeframe within which approved changes are to be implemented in the actual state. 3) A defect occurs when a device in the assessment boundary: a. includes a proposed change that has not been addressed within the time allowed in 2(a); or b. includes an approved change that has not been implemented within the timeframe specified in 2(b).	TBD by organization

Example Responses:

Defect Check ID	Potential Response Action	Primary Responsibility
SWAM-L03	Automatically block unapproved changes	ISCM-Ops
SWAM-L03	Automatically put into effect approved changes	SWMan
SWAM-L03	Manually remove unapproved changes promptly	SWMan
SWAM-L03	Manually implement approved changes promptly	SWMan
SWAM-L03	Change authorizations	Auth
SWAM-L03	Accept risk	RskEx
SWAM-L03	Oversee and coordinate response	DSM

Supporting Control Items:

Defect Check ID	Baseline	SP 800-53 Control Item Code
SWAM-L03	Low	SI-3(d)
SWAM-L03	Moderate	SI-3(2)
SWAM-L03	High	CM-3(1)(c)

3.2.3.4 Prevent or Reduce Exploitation of Software on Devices Moving into or out of Protective Boundaries *Sub-Capability and Defect Check SWAM-L04*

The purpose of this sub-capability is defined as follows:

Sub-Capability Name	Sub-Capability Purpose
Prevent or reduce exploitation of software on devices moving into or out of protective boundaries	Prevent exploitation of software on devices after removal, during use elsewhere, and after return (or other mobile use) by a) appropriately hardening the device prior to removal; b) checking for organizational software before removal; and c) sanitizing the device before introduction or reintroduction into the protective boundary. *Note:* For more information on media sanitization, see Kissel, R. et al (2014), Guidelines for Media Sanitization (National Institute of Standards and Technology, Gaithersburg, MD), NIST Special Publication (SP) 800-88, https://csrc.nist.gov/publications/detail/sp/800-88/rev-1/final.

The defect check to assess whether this sub-capability is operating effectively is defined as follows:

Defect Check ID	Defect Check Name	Assessment Criteria Notes	Selected
SWAM-L04	Devices moving in/out of protective boundaries not in policy compliance	1) The actual state includes: a. the actual installed software configuration on devices approved for travel (i.e., removal and reintroduction). This typically consists of the presence or absence of specific software. b. data identifying devices about to be used in travel (and to where). c. data identifying devices reentering protective boundaries (and where else the device has been connected while outside of protective boundaries. The locations might be validated from global positioning system (GPS) and internet protocol (IP) logging, if appropriate). 2) The desired state includes: a. the list of devices authorized for travel. b. the desired installed software strengthening (adding software protections and/or removing sensitive software) and/or sanitization (restoring software and/or finding and removing malicious software) for such devices, based on the location(s) to which connected while removed, with respect to 1a and 1c above. 3) A defect occurs when any of the following occur: a. any device unauthorized for travel is either expected to be (or has actually been) traveling, regardless of installed software configuration. b. a device approved for travel does not have the desired installed software configuration for the proposed uses. c. a device approved for travel was connected to unapproved location(s) where its installed software configuration was not appropriate (matching the desired state) for those location(s). d. a device approved and used for travel is not sanitized on its return based on the location(s) to which connected while outside of protective boundaries, with respect to items 1a and 1c above.	TBD by organization

Example Responses:

Defect Check ID	Potential Response Action	Primary Responsibility
SWAM-L04	Correct configurations before allowing exit from boundary	SWMan
SWAM-L04	Correct configurations before allowing entry to boundary	SWMan
SWAM-L04	Authorize the new state	Auth
SWAM-L04	Accept risk	RskEx
SWAM-L04	Oversee and coordinate response	DSM

Supporting Control Items:

Defect Check ID	Baseline	SP 800-53 Control Item Code
SWAM-L04	Low	CM-11(b)
SWAM-L04	Low	MP-6(a)
SWAM-L04	Low	MP-6(b)
SWAM-L04	Low	PS-4(d)
SWAM-L04	Low	SI-3(b)
SWAM-L04	Moderate	CM-2(7)(a)
SWAM-L04	Moderate	CM-2(7)(b)
SWAM-L04	Moderate	CM-7(1)(b)
SWAM-L04	Moderate	CM-7(4)(a)
SWAM-L04	Moderate	CM-7(4)(b)
SWAM-L04	Moderate	MA-3(1)
SWAM-L04	Moderate	MA-3(2)
SWAM-L04	High	CM-7(5)(a)
SWAM-L04	High	CM-7(5)(b)
SWAM-L04	High	MP-6(1)
SWAM-L04	High	MP-6(2)
SWAM-L04	High	MP-6(3)

3.2.3.5 Enable Rollback and Recovery Sub-Capability and Defect Check SWAM-L05

The purpose of this sub-capability is defined as follows:

Sub-Capability Name	Sub-Capability Purpose
Enable rollback and recovery	Require the maintenance of enough prior versions of software to ensure the ability to rollback and recover in the event that issues are found with the newer software.

The defect check to assess whether this sub-capability is operating effectively is defined as follows:

Defect Check ID	Defect Check Name	Assessment Criteria Notes	Selected
SWAM-L05	Number of prior versions of installed software inadequate	1) The actual state includes (for each device's software items): a. the number of prior versions (replaced version) maintained. b. the date each prior version was removed from the device. c. the date the oldest version was put in service on that device. 2) The desired state includes: a. the minimum number (n) of prior versions to be maintained. b. the minimum time (t) prior versions are to be maintained. 3) A defect occurs when a device is connected to the assessment boundary where less than the minimum number of prior versions of the software item have been retained. *Note 1:* The prior versions do not generally reside on the device itself, but typically on some backup media. *Note 2:* The number of required prior versions might be different for each software product or class of software products, as specified by the organization.	TBD by organization

Example Responses:

Defect Check ID	Potential Response Action	Primary Responsibility
SWAM-L05	Reconstruct backup version(s)	SWMan
SWAM-L05	Modify procedures to prevent future occurrences	RskEx
SWAM-L05	Change requirements	DSM
SWAM-L05	Accept risk	RskEx
SWAM-L05	Oversee and coordinate response	RskEx

Supporting Control Items:

Defect Check ID	Baseline	SP 800-53 Control Item Code
SWAM-L05	Moderate	CM-2(3)

3.2.3.6 Prevent or Reduce Software Defects *Sub-Capability and Defect Check SWAM-L06*

The purpose of this sub-capability is defined as follows:

Sub-Capability Name	Sub-Capability Purpose
Prevent or reduce software defects	Prevent or reduce the installation of software which has not been tested and validated prior to approval.

The defect check to assess whether this sub-capability is operating effectively is defined as follows:

Defect Check ID	Defect Check Name	Assessment Criteria Notes	Selected
SWAM-L06	Testing and validation of software inadequate	1) The actual state includes (for each software item on one or more devices): a. the testing and validation steps conducted for that software. b. the attributes of this software (used to determine the desired level of testing, see desired state). 2) The desired state includes: a. the organization defined software item attributes used to determine the correct amount and kind of testing and validation. b. the specification of the correct amount and kind of testing and validation for each combination of relevant attributes. 3) A defect occurs when a device connected to the assessment boundary has installed software where the amount and kind of testing and validation of the installed software is not at least as complete as the desired state specification for the software item's combination of relevant categories.	TBD by organization

Example Responses:

Defect Check ID	Potential Response Action	Primary Responsibility
SWAM-L06	Automatically block execution of software	ISCM-Ops
SWAM-L06	Remove the software	SWMan
SWAM-L06	Change testing and validation requirements	DSM
SWAM-L06	Accept risk	RskEx
SWAM-L06	Oversee and coordinate response	RskEx

LOCAL DEFECT CHECKS

Supporting Control Items:

Defect Check ID	Baseline	SP 800-53 Control Item Code
SWAM-L06	Low	CM-4
SWAM-L06	High	CM-4(1)

3.2.3.7 Verify Ongoing Business Need for Software *Sub-Capability and Defect Check SWAM-L07*

The purpose of this sub-capability is defined as follows:

Sub-Capability Name	Sub-Capability Purpose
Verify ongoing business need for software	Require periodic and/or event driven consideration of whether a software item is still needed for system functionality to fulfill mission requirements in support of least functionality). *Note:* Recommended practice is to require DMs to review devices for unauthorized, unneeded or unmanaged software, and System Owners to review what software is needed in the authorization boundaries, compared to what is present.

The defect check to assess whether this sub-capability is operating effectively is defined as follows:

Defect Check ID	Defect Check Name	Assessment Criteria Notes	Selected
SWAM-L07	Business need of software not recently verified	1) The actual state includes (for each software item): a. the date business need was last verified; and/or b. whether or not a specified trigger event has occurred. 2) The desired state includes: a. the maximum time before re-verification is required for each software item. b. a software item sunset date and/or specific trigger events requiring consideration of software item relevance, i. by device type and/or software item role/attributes. ii. by device type and/or software item identity. 3) A defect occurs when a device connected to the assessment boundary: a. has a software item with an expired sunset date; or b. has a software item nearing an expired sunset date (to provide warning to desired state managers); or c. a specified trigger event has occurred to this device or software item without re-verification of business need.	TBD by organization

LOCAL DEFECT CHECKS

Example Responses:

Defect Check ID	Potential Response Action	Primary Responsibility
SWAM-L07	Verify business need	Auth
SWAM-L07	Automatically block execution of software	ISCM-Ops
SWAM-L07	Remove the software	SWMan
SWAM-L07	Change requirement for verification of business need	DSM
SWAM-L07	Accept risk	RskEx
SWAM-L07	Oversee and coordinate response	RskEx

Supporting Control Items:

Defect Check ID	Baseline	SP 800-53 Control Item Code
SWAM-L07	Low	CM-4
SWAM-L07	Low	CM-7(a)
SWAM-L07	Moderate	CM-7(1)(a)
SWAM-L07	Moderate	CM-7(4)(c)
SWAM-L07	High	CM-7(5)(c)

3.2.3.8 Prevent or Reduce Unused (and thus Unneeded) Software Products *Sub-Capability and Defect Check SWAM-L08*

The purpose of this sub-capability is defined as follows:

Sub-Capability Name	Sub-Capability Purpose
Prevent or reduce unused (and thus unneeded) software products	Prevent or reduce the presence of unused (and thus unneeded) software products as determined by actual usage on a given device.

The defect check to assess whether this sub-capability is operating effectively is defined as follows:

Defect Check ID	Defect Check Name	Assessment Criteria Notes	Selected
SWAM-L08	Unused software present	1) The actual state includes (for each software product on one or more devices): a. actual software product attributes (see note) used to determine how much it is expected to be used. b. the last date of use. c. the number of times used in an organizationally defined period. 2) The desired state includes: a. the software product attributes (see note) used to determine the expected amount of use. b) the specification of the expected amount of use for each combination of relevant categories. 3) A defect occurs when a device connected to the assessment boundary has installed software products where any of the following are true: a) the last use is older than expected. b) the rate of use is less than expected. *Note for 1a and 2a:* Different or variable timeframes/usage patterns for different types and classes of software might be needed, since some software might be used at differing frequencies. For example, some "quarterly report software" might only be expected to be used quarterly, while "annual report software" might only be used annually.	TBD by organization

LOCAL DEFECT CHECKS

Example Responses:

Defect Check ID	Potential Response Action	Primary Responsibility
SWAM-L08	Remove the software	SWMan
SWAM-L08	Change usage expectations	DSM
SWAM-L08	Accept risk	RskEx
SWAM-L08	Oversee and coordinate response	RskEx

Supporting Control Items:

Defect Check ID	Baseline	SP 800-53 Control Item Code
SWAM-L08	Low	CM-4
SWAM-L08	Low	CM-7(a)
SWAM-L08	Moderate	CM-7(1)(a)

3.2.3.9 Ensure Software Is Required by a System *Sub-Capability and Defect Check SWAM-L09*

The purpose of this sub-capability is defined as follows:

Sub-Capability Name	Sub-Capability Purpose
Ensure device-software-item level accountability	Ensure each unique combination of a device and software item (device-software-item) has accountability. Reduce duplication of effort by verifying that each unique combination of device and software-item is in one and only one authorization boundary.
	Note: For this defect check, the relevant software item is more likely a software product than a software file.

The defect check to assess whether this sub-capability is operating effectively is defined as follows:

Defect Check ID	Defect Check Name	Assessment Criteria Notes	Selected
SWAM-L09	Device-software-item assignment to authorization boundary is not 1:1	1) The actual state includes the authorization boundary(ies) to which the device-software-item combination is assigned in the desired state. 2) The desired state is that each device-software-item combination is in one and only one authorization boundary, and thus has a clearly defined management responsibility. 3) A defect occurs when an actual state device-software-item combination is: a. not listed in any authorization boundary; or b. listed in more than one authorization boundary. *Note:* For guidance on defining authorization boundaries, see NIST SP 800-37.	TBD by organization

Example Responses:

Defect Check ID	Potential Response Action	Primary Responsibility
SWAM-L09	Block the software	ISCM-Ops
SWAM-L09	Remove the software	SWMan
SWAM-L09	Adjust authorization boundary assignment	DSM
SWAM-L09	Accept risk	RskEx
SWAM-L09	Oversee and coordinate response	RskEx

Supporting Control Items:

Defect Check ID	Baseline	SP 800-53 Control Item Code
SWAM-L09	Low	CM-11(b)
SWAM-L09	Moderate	CM-8(5)

3.2.3.10 Ensure that Software Complies with License Agreements *Sub-Capability and Defect Check SWAM-L10*

The purpose of this sub-capability is defined as follows:

Sub-Capability Name	Sub-Capability Purpose
Ensure that software complies with license agreements	Ensure that actual usage of software products complies with license agreements.

The defect check to assess whether this sub-capability is operating effectively is defined as follows:

Defect Check ID	Defect Check Name	Assessment Criteria Notes	Selected
SWAM-L10	Unlicensed software	1) The actual state includes a) the inventory of each unique combination of a device and software product (device-software-products) installed. b) data (such as number installed, numbers concurrently used, amount of use, copies of installation media, protection of media) to determine the extent of license compliance for each software product. 2) The desired state includes the criteria (such as number allowed to be installed, number concurrently allowed to be used, limits to installation on specific devices, and amount of use) needed to determine license compliance for each software product. 3) A defect occurs when the actual state of a software-product is not in compliance with the desired state. For example: a. the criteria in 2) might be that 80 copies may be installed, but the actual state of 1.a) is that 85 are installed b) the criteria in 2) might limit concurrent users to 100, but the actual state in 1.b) might indicate that there are periods with up to 125 concurrent users. c) The criteria in 2) might limit hours of use to 1000, but the actual state in 1.b) might indicate that 1010 hours were used. *Note 1:* The criteria in 2) might limit the use of installation media to organizationally owned devices, but 1) and 2) might be expanded to indicate that such media have been distributed to be used on other devices. *Note 2:* The object of assessment for SWAM-L10 is the software product and its licensed usage, not individual devices or endpoints.	TBD by organization

LOCAL DEFECT CHECKS

Example Responses:

Defect Check ID	Potential Response Action	Primary Responsibility
SWAM-L10	Block the software	ISCM-Ops
SWAM-L10	Remove the software	SWMan
SWAM-L10	Obtain/Renew the license	SWMan
SWAM-L10	Adjust usage	DSM
SWAM-L10	Accept risk	RskEx
SWAM-L10	Oversee and coordinate response	RskEx

Supporting Control Items:

Defect Check ID	Baseline	SP 800-53 Control Item Code
SWAM-L10	Low	CM-4
SWAM-L10	Low	CM-10(a)
SWAM-L10	Low	CM-10(b)
SWAM-L10	Low	CM-10(c)
SWAM-L10	Low	CM-11(b)

3.2.3.11 Required Software Is Present *Sub-Capability and Defect Check SWAM-L11*

The purpose of this sub-capability is defined as follows:

Sub-Capability Name	Sub-Capability Purpose
Required software is present	Avoid denial of service from missing required software.

The defect check to assess whether this sub-capability is operating effectively is defined as follows:

Defect Check ID	Defect Check Name	Assessment Criteria Notes	Selected
SWAM-L11	Required software not present	1) The actual state includes the inventory of software present on the device(s). 2) The desired state includes the list of required software for the device(s). 3) A defect occurs when a software item is required and not present.	TBD by organization

Example Responses:

Defect Check ID	Potential Response Action	Primary Responsibility
SWAM-L11	Install missing required software	SWMan
SWAM-L11	Remove requirement	DSM
SWAM-L11	Accept risk	RskEx
SWAM-L11	Oversee and coordinate response	RskEx

Supporting Control Items:

Defect Check ID	Baseline	SP 800-53 Control Item Code
SWAM-L11	Low	CM-2
SWAM-L11	Low	CM-8(a)
SWAM-L11	Low	CM-8(b)
SWAM-L11	Moderate	CM-2(1)(a)
SWAM-L11	Moderate	CM-2(1)(b)
SWAM-L11	Moderate	CM-2(1)(c)
SWAM-L11	Moderate	CM-8(1)

3.2.3.12 Ensure that Software is Managed Sub-Capability and Defect Check SWAM-L12

The purpose of this sub-capability is defined as follows:

Sub-Capability Name	Sub-Capability Purpose
Ensure that software is managed	Ensure clear responsibility for software change implementation to facilitate the presence of only the authorized software for the device. *Note:* Patching can be done with a security purpose and/or a functional purpose. When a patch is applied for security purposes, it is explicitly covered under the Vulnerability Management capability, because of the extra risk created by security vulnerabilities. Patching for changes to functionality is addressed by SWAM-L12.

The defect check to assess whether this sub-capability is operating effectively is defined as follows:

Defect Check ID	Defect Check Name	Assessment Criteria Notes	Selected

SWAM-L12	Unmanaged software	1) The actual state is the list of software product installation managers assigned to manage each installed software product (and/or to remove unauthorized products) on each device.
		2) The desired state specification the list of approved software product installation managers for:
		  a. each software product type or product; and
		  b. each device type or device.
		3) A defect is an authorized installed software product where
		  a. no software product installation manager is specified, or
		  b. the specified software product installation manager is not authorized for that software product (or type) on that device (or type).
		
		Note: The SWAM-F01, SWAM-F02, and SWAM-F03 status must be known to assess HWAM-F02, in order to avoid requiring an installer account for unauthorized software.
			TBD by organization

Example Responses:

Defect Check ID	Potential Response Action	Primary Responsibility
SWAM-L12	Block the software	ISCM-Ops
SWAM-L12	Remove the software when no SWMan assigned	DM
SWAM-L12	Assign an appropriate SWMan	Auth
SWAM-L12	Accept risk	RskEx
SWAM-L12	Oversee and coordinate response	DSM

Supporting Control Items:

Defect Check ID	Baseline	SP 800-53 Control Item Code
SWAM-L12	Low	CM-11(b)
SWAM-L12	High	CM-8(4)

3.2.3.13 Increase Software Maintainability and Integrity *Sub-Capability and Defect Check SWAM-L13*

The purpose of this sub-capability is defined as follows:

Sub-Capability Name	Sub-Capability Purpose
Increase software maintainability and integrity	Ensures that only software with warranty and/or source code is authorized so that it can be maintained.

The defect check to assess whether this sub-capability is operating effectively is defined as follows:

Defect Check ID	Defect Check Name	Assessment Criteria Notes	Selected
SWAM-L13	Software without warranty and/or source code	1) The actual state includes, for each software product installed on at least one device in the assessment boundary the availability of (based on having such items under configuration management): a. source code for the product. b. a general warranty for the product. c. a commitment to find and fix security defects for the product and information about the software product necessary to determine which of the preceding items is required for that product (e.g., whether software is commercial-off-the-shelf (COTS), government-off-the-shelf (GOTS), or custom software). 2) The desired state includes: the criteria (needed to determine whether source code and/or specific warranty terms are required for a software product. 3) A defect occurs when a software-product's nature requires the organization to have source code and or specific warranty terms, which the software product does not provide.	TBD by organization

LOCAL DEFECT CHECKS

Example Responses:

Defect Check ID	Potential Response Action	Primary Responsibility
SWAM-L13	Automatically block execution of software	ISCM-Ops
SWAM-L13	Manually remove the software	SWMan
SWAM-L13	Obtain the missing warranty, documentation, etc.	RskEx
SWAM-L13	Accept risk	RskEx
SWAM-L13	Oversee and coordinate response	DSM

Supporting Control Items:

Defect Check ID	Baseline	SP 800-53 Control Item Code
SWAM-L13	Low	CM-4
SWAM-L13	Low	CM-11(b)
SWAM-L13	High	SI-7(14)(a)

3.2.3.14 Prevent or Reduce Malware Sub-Capability and Defect Check SWAM-L14

The purpose of this sub-capability is defined as follows:

Sub-Capability Name	Sub-Capability Purpose
Prevent or reduce malware	Ensures that black-listing methods such as anti-virus protection and spam filters are in place to block the most obvious sources of malware, as judged needed by the organization.

The defect check to assess whether this sub-capability is operating effectively is defined as follows:

Defect Check ID	Defect Check Name	Assessment Criteria Notes	Selected
SWAM-L14	Poor anti-virus (AV) protection	1) The actual state is the: a. list of software blacklisting products or mechanisms operating. b. the kinds of operations they are doing. c. the date the blacklist was last updated. 2) The desired state specification the list of approved software product installation managers for: a. list of software blacklisting products or mechanisms expected to be operating. b. the kinds of operations they are expected to be doing. c. the expected frequency with which they are to be updated. 3) A defect is a blacklisting product or mechanism: a. expected to be present, but which is not; or b. not performing its expected operations; or c. not last updated within the expected frequency.	TBD by organization

Example Responses:

Defect Check ID	Potential Response Action	Primary Responsibility
SWAM-L14	Install Blacklisting solutions where missing	SWMan
SWAM-L14	Remove the requirement	DSM
SWAM-L14	Accept risk	RskEx
SWAM-L14	Oversee and coordinate response	RskEx

LOCAL DEFECT CHECKS

Supporting Control Items:

Defect Check ID	Baseline	SP 800-53 Control Item Code
SWAM-L14	Low	CM-4
SWAM-L14	Low	SI-3(a)
SWAM-L14	Low	SI-3(b)
SWAM-L14	Low	SI-3(c)

3.2.4 Security Impact of Each Sub-Capability on an Attack Step Model

Table 6 shows the primary ways the defect checks derived from the SP 800-53 security controls contribute to blocking attacks/events as described in Figure 1: SWAM Impact on an Attack Step Model.

Table 6: Mapping of Attack Steps to Security Sub-Capability

Attack Step	Attack Step Description	Sub-Capability ID and Name	Sub-Capability Purpose
1) Gain Internal Entry	The attacker is outside the target boundaries and seeks entry. Examples include: spear phishing email sent; DDoS attack against .gov initiated. Unauthorized person attempts to gain physical access to restricted facility.	SWAM-L04: Prevent or reduce exploitation of software on devices moving into or out of protective boundaries	Prevent exploitation of software on devices after removal, during use elsewhere, and after return (or other mobile use) by a) appropriately hardening the device prior to removal; b) checking for organizational software before removal; and c) sanitizing the device before introduction or reintroduction into the protective boundary. *Note:* For more information on sanitization, see NIST SP 800-88, Guidelines for Media Sanitization.
1) Gain Internal Entry	The attacker is outside the target boundaries and seeks entry. Examples include: spear phishing email sent; DDoS attack against .gov initiated. Unauthorized person attempts to gain physical access to restricted facility.	SWAM-L06: Prevent or reduce software defects	Prevent or reduce the installation of software which has not been tested and validated prior to approval.
1) Gain Internal Entry	The attacker is outside the target boundaries and seeks entry. Examples include: spear phishing email sent; DDoS attack against .gov initiated. Unauthorized person attempts to gain physical access to restricted facility.	SWAM-L12: Ensure that software is managed	Ensure clear responsibility for software change implementation to facilitate the presence of only the authorized software for the device.

Attack Step	Attack Step Description	Sub-Capability ID and Name	Sub-Capability Purpose
3) Gain Foothold	The attacker has gained entry to the assessment object and achieves enough compromise to gain a foothold, but without persistence. Examples include: Unauthorized user successfully logs in with authorized credentials; browser exploit code successfully executed in memory and initiates call back; person gains unauthorized access to server room.	SWAM-F01: Prevent unauthorized software from executing	Prevent or reduce the execution of unauthorized software (presumed malware).
3) Gain Foothold	The attacker has gained entry to the assessment object and achieves enough compromise to gain a foothold, but without persistence. Examples include: Unauthorized user successfully logs in with authorized credentials; browser exploit code successfully executed in memory and initiates call back; person gains unauthorized access to server room.	SWAM-F02: Prevent or reduce execution of software from unauthorized installers	Prevent or reduce the execution of software (presumed malware) installed by an unauthorized installer.
3) Gain Foothold	The attacker has gained entry to the assessment object and achieves enough compromise to gain a foothold, but without persistence. Examples include: Unauthorized user successfully logs in with authorized credentials; browser exploit code successfully executed in memory and initiates call back; person gains unauthorized access to server room.	SWAM-L01: Ensure or increase integrity of software authorizers	Prevent or reduce the insertion of malware into the list of approved software by unauthorized persons.
3) Gain Foothold	The attacker has gained entry to the assessment object and achieves enough compromise to gain a foothold, but without persistence. Examples include: Unauthorized user successfully logs in with authorized credentials; browser exploit code successfully executed in memory and initiates call back; person gains unauthorized access to server room.	SWAM-L02: Prevent or reduce (careless or malicious) software approval	Ensure checks and balances are in place to prevent a single individual from carelessly or maliciously changing authorization of software installation. Note 1: If the organization chooses to use access restrictions to enforce multiple approvals, effectiveness is assessed under the PRIV capability. Note 2: See SWAM-L09 for authorization boundary.

Attack Step	Attack Step Description	Sub-Capability ID and Name	Sub-Capability Purpose
3) Gain Foothold	The attacker has gained entry to the assessment object and achieves enough compromise to gain a foothold, but without persistence. Examples include: Unauthorized user successfully logs in with authorized credentials; browser exploit code successfully executed in memory and initiates call back; person gains unauthorized access to server room.	SWAM-L06: Prevent or reduce software defects	Prevent or reduce the installation of software which has not been tested and validated prior to approval.
3) Gain Foothold	The attacker has gained entry to the assessment object and achieves enough compromise to gain a foothold, but without persistence. Examples include: Unauthorized user successfully logs in with authorized credentials; browser exploit code successfully executed in memory and initiates call back; person gains unauthorized access to server room.	SWAM-L07: Verify ongoing business need for software	Require periodic and/or event driven consideration of whether a software item is still needed for system functionality to fulfill mission requirements in support of least functionality). *Note:* Recommended practice is to require DMs to review devices for unauthorized, unneeded or unmanaged software, ard System Owners to review what software is needed in the authorization boundaries, compared to what is present.
3) Gain Foothold	The attacker has gained entry to the assessment object and achieves enough compromise to gain a foothold, but without persistence. Examples include: Unauthorized user successfully logs in with authorized credentials; browser exploit code successfully executed in memory and initiates call back; person gains unauthorized access to server room.	SWAM-L08: Prevent or reduce unused (and thus unneeded) software products	Prevent or reduce the presence of unused (and thus unneeded) software products as determined by actual usage on a given device.
3) Gain Foothold	The attacker has gained entry to the assessment object and achieves enough compromise to gain a foothold, but without persistence. Examples include: Unauthorized user successfully logs in with authorized credentials; browser exploit code successfully executed in memory and initiates call back; person gains unauthorized access to server room.	SWAM-L13: Increase software maintainability and integrity	Ensures that only software with warranty and/or source code is authorized so that it can be maintained.

Attack Step	Attack Step Description	Sub-Capability ID and Name	Sub-Capability Purpose
4) Gain Persistence	The attack has gained a foothold on the object and now achieves persistence. Examples include: Malware installed on host that survives reboot or log off; BIOS or kernel modified; new/privileged account created for unauthorized user; unauthorized person issued credentials/allowed access; unauthorized personnel added to access control list (ACL) for server room.	SWAM-F02: Prevent or reduce execution of software from unauthorized installers	Prevent or reduce the execution of software (presumed malware) installed by an unauthorized installer.
4) Gain Persistence	The attack has gained a foothold on the object and now achieves persistence. Examples include: Malware installed on host that survives reboot or log off; BIOS or kernel modified; new/privileged account created for unauthorized user; unauthorized person issued credentials/allowed access; unauthorized personnel added to access control list (ACL) for server room.	SWAM-F03: Prevent or reduce software execution from unauthorized location	Prevent or reduce the execution of software (presumed malware) loaded from an uncontrolled or unauthorized location.
4) Gain Persistence	The attack has gained a foothold on the object and now achieves persistence. Examples include: Malware installed on host that survives reboot or log off; BIOS or kernel modified; new/privileged account created for unauthorized user; unauthorized person issued credentials/allowed access; unauthorized personnel added to access control list (ACL) for server room.	SWAM-F04: Ensure or increase trust of system software at startup	Prevent or reduce the insertion of malware into key system components before or during system startup.
4) Gain Persistence	The attack has gained a foothold on the object and now achieves persistence. Examples include: Malware installed on host that survives reboot or log off; BIOS or kernel modified; new/privileged account created for unauthorized user; unauthorized person issued credentials/allowed access; unauthorized personnel added to access control list (ACL) for server room.	SWAM-L01: Ensure or increase integrity of software authorizers	Prevent or reduce the insertion of malware into the list of approved software by unauthorized persons.

Attack Step	Attack Step Description	Sub-Capability ID and Name	Sub-Capability Purpose
4) Gain Persistence	The attack has gained a foothold on the object and now achieves persistence. Examples include: Malware installed on host that survives reboot or log off; BIOS or kernel modified; new/privileged account created for unauthorized user; unauthorized person issued credentials/allowed access; unauthorized personnel added to access control list (ACL) for server room.	SWAM-L02: Prevent or reduce (careless or malicious) software approval	Ensure checks and balances are in place to prevent a single individual from carelessly or maliciously changing authorization of software installation. *Note 1:* If the organization chooses to use access restrictions to enforce multiple approvals, effectiveness is assessed under the PRIV capability. *Note 2:* See SWAM-L09 for authorization boundary.
4) Gain Persistence	The attack has gained a foothold on the object and now achieves persistence. Examples include: Malware installed on host that survives reboot or log off; BIOS or kernel modified; new/privileged account created for unauthorized user; unauthorized person issued credentials/allowed access; unauthorized personnel added to access control list (ACL) for server room.	SWAM-L03: Promptly determine and address needed installation and deinstallation of software	Ensure that needed changes are addressed in a timely manner by flagging requested changes not considered (approved and implemented; or disapproved) in a timely manner as risks.
4) Gain Persistence	The attack has gained a foothold on the object and now achieves persistence. Examples include: Malware installed on host that survives reboot or log off; BIOS or kernel modified; new/privileged account created for unauthorized user; unauthorized person issued credentials/allowed access; unauthorized personnel added to access control list (ACL) for server room.	SWAM-L07: Verify ongoing business need for software	Require periodic and/or event driven consideration of whether a software item is still needed for system functionality to fulfill mission requirements in support of least functionality). *Note:* Recommended practice is to require DMs to review devices for unauthorized, unneeded or unmanaged software, and System Owners to review what software is needed in the authorization boundaries, compared to what is present.

Attack Step	Attack Step Description	Sub-Capability ID and Name	Sub-Capability Purpose
4) Gain Persistence	The attack has gained a foothold on the object and now achieves persistence. Examples include: Malware installed on host that survives reboot or log off; BIOS or kernel modified; new/privileged account created for unauthorized user; unauthorized person issued credentials/allowed access; unauthorized personnel added to access control list (ACL) for server room.	SWAM-L08: Prevent or reduce unused (and thus unneeded) software products	Prevent or reduce the presence of unused (and thus unneeded) software products as determined by actual usage on a given device.
4) Gain Persistence	The attack has gained a foothold on the object and now achieves persistence. Examples include: Malware installed on host that survives reboot or log off; BIOS or kernel modified; new/privileged account created for unauthorized user; unauthorized person issued credentials/allowed access; unauthorized personnel added to access control list (ACL) for server room.	SWAM-L09: Ensure device-software-item level accountability	Ensure each unique combination of a device and software item (device-software-item) has accountability. Reduce duplication of effort by verifying that each unique combination of device and software-item is in one and only one authorization boundary.

Note: For this defect check, the relevant software item is more likely a software product than a software file. |
| 4) Gain Persistence | The attack has gained a foothold on the object and now achieves persistence. Examples include: Malware installed on host that survives reboot or log off; BIOS or kernel modified; new/privileged account created for unauthorized user; unauthorized person issued credentials/allowed access; unauthorized personnel added to access control list (ACL) for server room. | SWAM-L10: Ensure that software complies with license agreements | Ensure that actual usage of software products complies with license agreements. |

Attack Step	Attack Step Description	Sub-Capability ID and Name	Sub-Capability Purpose
4) Gain Persistence	The attack has gained a foothold on the object and now achieves persistence. Examples include: Malware installed on host that survives reboot or log off; BIOS or kernel modified; new/privileged account created for unauthorized user; unauthorized person issued credentials/allowed access; unauthorized personnel added to access control list (ACL) for server room.	SWAM-L12: Ensure that software is managed	Ensure clear responsibility for software change implementation to facilitate the presence of only the authorized software for the device.
4) Gain Persistence	The attack has gained a foothold on the object and now achieves persistence. Examples include: Malware installed on host that survives reboot or log off; BIOS or kernel modified; new/privileged account created for unauthorized user; unauthorized person issued credentials/allowed access; unauthorized personnel added to access control list (ACL) for server room.	SWAM-L13: Increase software maintainability and integrity	Ensures that only software with warranty and/or source code is authorized so that it can be maintained.
4) Gain Persistence	The attack has gained a foothold on the object and now achieves persistence. Examples include: Malware installed on host that survives reboot or log off; BIOS or kernel modified; new/privileged account created for unauthorized user; unauthorized person issued credentials/allowed access; unauthorized personnel added to access control list (ACL) for server room.	SWAM-L14: Prevent or reduce malware	Ensures that black-listing methods such as anti-virus protection and spam filters are in place to block the most obvious sources of malware, as judged needed by the organization.
6) Achieve Attack Objective	The attacker achieves an objective. Loss of confidentiality, integrity, or availability of data or system capability. Examples include: Exfiltration of files; modification of database entries; deletion of file or application; denial of service; disclosure of PII.	SWAM-L05: Enable rollback and recovery	Require the maintenance of enough prior versions of software to ensure the ability to rollback and recover in the event that issues are found with the newer software.

Attack Step	Attack Step Description	Sub-Capability ID and Name	Sub-Capability Purpose
6) Achieve Attack Objective	The attacker achieves an objective. Loss of confidentiality, integrity, or availability of data or system capability. Examples include: Exfiltration of files; modification of database entries; deletion of file or application; denial of service; disclosure of PII.	SWAM-L10: Ensure that software complies with license agreements	Ensure that actual usage of software products complies with license agreements.
6) Achieve Attack Objective	The attacker achieves an objective. Loss of confidentiality, integrity, or availability of data or system capability. Examples include: Exfiltration of files; modification of database entries; deletion of file or application; denial of service; disclosure of PII.	SWAM-L11: Required software is present	Avoid self-denial of service from missing required software.

3.3 SWAM Control (Item) Security Assessment Plan Narrative Tables and Templates

The security assessment plan narratives in this section are designed to provide the core of an assessment plan for the automated assessment, as described in Section 6 of Volume 1 of this NISTIR. The narratives are supplemented by the other material in this section, including defect check tables (defining the tests to be used) and are summarized in the Control Allocation Tables in Section 3.4.

The roles referenced in the narratives match the roles defined by NIST in relevant special publications (SP 800-37, etc.) and/or the SWAM-specific roles defined in Section 2.7. The roles can be adapted and/or customized to the organization as described in the introduction to Section 3.

The determination statements listed here have been derived from the relevant control item language, specifically modified by the following adjustments:

(1) The phrase {software} has been added where necessary for control items that apply to more areas than just SWAM. This language tailors the control item to remain within SWAM. In this case, the same control item is likely to appear in other capabilities with the relevant scoping for that capability. For example, most Configuration Management (CM) family controls apply not only to hardware CM, but also to software CM. Only the software CM aspect is relevant to the SWAM capability, so that is what is covered in this volume.

(2) The phrases {actual state} or {desired state specification} have been added to determination statements where both actual and desired state are needed for automated testing but where this was implicit in the original statement of the control. For example, CM-8a has two determination statements that are identical except that determination statement CM-8a(1) applies to the actual state, and determination statement CM-8a(2) applies to the desired state specification.

(3) Where a control item includes inherently different actions that are best assessed by different defect checks (typically, because the assessment criteria are different), the control item may be divided into multiple SWAM-applicable determination statements.

(4) Part of a control item may not apply to SWAM, while another part does. To address this issue, the determination statements in this volume include only the portion of the control item applicable to the SWAM capability. The portion of the control item that does not apply is documented by a note under the control item and included with other capabilities, as appropriate.

3.3.1 Outline Followed for Each Control Item

The literal text of the control item follows the heading *Control Item Text*.

There may be one or more determination statements for each control item. Each determination statement is documented in a table, noting the:

- determination statement ID (Control Item ID concatenated with the Determination Statement Number, where Determination Number is enclosed in curly brackets);
- determination statement text;
- implemented by (responsibility);
- assessment boundary;
- assessment responsibility;
- assessment method;
- selected column (TBD by the organization);
- rationale for risk acceptance (thresholds) (TBD by the organization);
- frequency of assessment;[27] and
- impact of not implementing the defect check (TBD by the organization).

The determination statement details are followed by a table showing the defect checks (and related sub-capability) that might be caused to fail if the control being tested fails.

The resulting text provides a template for the organization to edit, as described in Section 3.1.

3.3.2 Outline Organized by Baselines

This section includes security control items selected in the SP 800-53 Low, Moderate, and High baselines and that support the SWAM capability. For convenience, the control items are presented in three sections as follows:

(1) **Low Baseline Control Items** (Section 3.3.3). Security control items in the low baseline, which are required for all systems.

(2) **Moderate Baseline Control Items** (Section 3.3.4). Security control items in the moderate baseline, which are also required for the high baseline.

(3) **High Baseline Control Items** (Section 3.3.5). Security control items that are required only for the high baseline.

Table 7 illustrates the applicability of the security control items to each baseline.

---

[27] While automated tools may be able to assess as frequently as every 3 to 4 days, organizations determine the appropriate assessment frequency in accordance with the ISCM strategy.

Table 7: Applicability of Control Items

FIPS-199[a] (SP 800-60)[b] System Impact Level	(1) Low Control Items (Section 3.3.3)	(2) Moderate Control Items (Section 3.3.4)	(3) High Control Items (Section 3.3.5)
Low	Applicable		
Moderate	Applicable	Applicable	
High	Applicable	Applicable	Applicable

[a] FIPS-199 defines Low, Moderate, and High overall potential impact designations.
[b] See SP 800-60, Section 3.2.

3.3.3 Low Baseline Security Control Item Narratives

3.3.3.1 Control Item CM-2: BASELINE CONFIGURATION

Control Item Text

Control: The organization develops, documents, and maintains under configuration control, a current baseline configuration of the information system.

Determination Statement 1

Determination Statement ID	Determination Statement Text
CM-2{1}	Determine if the organization: develops, documents, and maintains under configuration control, a current baseline configuration of the information system.

Roles and Assessment Methods

Determination Statement ID	Implemented By	Assessment Boundary	Assessment Responsibility	Assessment Methods	Selected	Rationale for Risk Acceptance	Frequency of Assessment	Impact of Not Implementing
CM-2{1}	DSM	ISCM-TN	ISCM-Sys	Test				

Defect Check Rationale Table

A failure in effectiveness of this control item results in a defect in one or more of the following defect checks:

Determination Statement ID	Defect Check ID	Defect Check Name	Rationale
CM-2{1}	SWAM-L11	Required software not present	If an [organization-defined measure] for this defect check is above [the organization-defined threshold], then defects in **developing, documenting, and maintaining under configuration control a current baseline configuration of the information system** related to this control item might be the cause of the defect, i.e., …. absence of required software.

3.3.3.2 Control Item CM-4: SECURITY IMPACT ANALYSIS

Control Item Text

Control: The organization analyzes changes to the information system to determine potential security impacts prior to change implementation.

Determination Statement 1

Determination Statement ID	Determination Statement Text
CM-4{1}	Determine if the organization: analyzes changes to the information system {software} to determine potential security impacts prior to change implementation.

Roles and Assessment Methods

Determination Statement ID	Implemented By	Assessment Boundary	Assessment Responsibility	Assessment Methods	Selected	Rationale for Risk Acceptance	Frequency of Assessment	Impact of Not Implementing
CM-4{1}	DSM	ISCM-TN	ISCM-Sys	Test				

Defect Check Rationale Table

A failure in effectiveness of this control item results in a defect in one or more of the following defect checks:

Determination Statement ID	Defect Check ID	Defect Check Name	Rationale If an [organization-defined measure] for this defect check is above [the organization-defined threshold], then defects in analyzing changes to the information system {software} to determine potential security impacts prior to change implementation related to this control item might be the cause of the defect, i.e., …
CM-4{1}	SWAM-L01	Unapproved authorizer	lack of verification that software was authorized by approved accounts (persons).
CM-4{1}	SWAM-L02	Required authorizations missing	careless or malicious authorization of software.
CM-4{1}	SWAM-L06	Testing and validation of software inadequate	lack of adequate testing and validation.
CM-4{1}	SWAM-L07	Business need of software not recently verified	the presence of software without a recently verified need, resulting in an increase in the attack surface without associated organizational value.
CM-4{1}	SWAM-L08	Unused software present	the presence of unneeded software, resulting in an increase in the attack surface.
CM-4{1}	SWAM-L10	Unlicensed software	use of software not in compliance with quantity licenses, contract agreements, or copyright laws.
CM-4{1}	SWAM-L13	Software without warranty and/or source code	the presence of software without warranty and/or source code.
CM-4{1}	SWAM-L14	Poor AV protection	absence of methods to block malware.

3.3.3.3 Control Item CM-7(a): LEAST FUNCTIONALITY

Control Item Text

Control: The organization:

a. Configures the information system to provide only essential capabilities.

Determination Statement 1

Determination Statement ID	Determination Statement Text
CM-7(a){1}	Determine if the organization: configures the system {installed software} to provide only essential capabilities.

Roles and Assessment Methods

Determination Statement ID	Implemented By	Assessment Boundary	Assessment Responsibility	Assessment Methods	Selected	Rationale for Risk Acceptance	Frequency of Assessment	Impact of Not Implementing
CM-7(a){1}	DSM	ISCM-TN	ISCM-Sys	Test				

Defect Check Rationale Table

A failure in effectiveness of this control item results in a defect in one or more of the following defect checks:

Determination Statement ID	Defect Check ID	Defect Check Name	Rationale
			If an [organization-defined measure] for this defect check is above [the organization-defined threshold], then defects in **configuring the system {installed software} to provide only essential capabilities** related to this control item might be the cause of the defect, i.e., ….
CM-7(a){1}	SWAM-L07	Business need of software not recently verified	the presence of software without a recently verified need, resulting in an increase in the attack surface without associated organizational value.
CM-7(a){1}	SWAM-L08	Unused software present	the presence of unneeded software, resulting in an increase in the attack surface.

3.3.3.4 Control Item CM-7(b): LEAST FUNCTIONALITY

Control Item Text

Control: The organization:

b. Prohibits or restricts the use of the following functions, ports, protocols, and/or services: [Assignment: organization-defined prohibited or restricted functions, ports, protocols, and/or services].

Determination Statement 1

Determination Statement ID	Determination Statement Text
CM-7(b){1}	Determine if the organization: prohibits or restricts the use of the following {installed software} functions and/or services: [Assignment: organization-defined prohibited or restricted functions and/or services].

Roles and Assessment Methods

Determination Statement ID	Implemented By	Assessment Boundary	Assessment Responsibility	Assessment Methods	Selected	Rationale for Risk Acceptance	Frequency of Assessment	Impact of Not Implementing
CM-7(b){1}	DSM	ISCM-TN	ISCM-Sys	Test				

Defect Check Rationale Table

A failure in effectiveness of this control item results in a defect in one or more of the following defect checks:

Determination Statement ID	Defect Check ID	Defect Check Name	Rationale
			If an [organization-defined measure] for this defect check is above [the organization-defined threshold], then defects in **prohibiting or restricting the use of specified {installed software} functions and/or services** related to this control item might be the cause of the defect, i.e., ….
CM-7(b){1}	SWAM-F01	Unauthorized software executes	the execution of unauthorized software.
CM-7(b){1}	SWAM-F03	Unauthorized software directory/folder location	the execution of software not loaded from an approved directory/folder location.

3.3.3.5 Control Item CM-8(a): INFORMATION SYSTEM COMPONENT INVENTORY

Control Item Text

Control: The organization:

a. Develops and documents an inventory of information system components that:

    1. Accurately reflects the current information system;

    2. Includes all components within the authorization boundary of the information system;

    3. Is at the level of granularity deemed necessary for tracking and reporting; and

    4. Includes [Assignment: organization-defined information deemed necessary to achieve effective information system component accountability].

Determination Statement 1

Determination Statement ID	Determination Statement Text
CM-8(a){1}	Determine if the organization: develops and documents an inventory of system components {for software} that: (1) accurately reflects the current system; and (2) includes all components within the authorization boundary of the system.

Roles and Assessment Methods

Determination Statement ID	Implemented By	Assessment Boundary	Assessment Responsibility	Assessment Methods	Selected	Rationale for Risk Acceptance	Frequency of Assessment	Impact of Not Implementing
CM-8(a){1}	DSM	ISCM-TN	ISCM-Sys	Test				

Defect Check Rationale Table

A failure in effectiveness of this control item results in a defect in one or more of the following defect checks:

Determination Statement ID	Defect Check ID	Defect Check Name	Rationale
CM-8(a){1}	SWAM-L11	Required software not present	If an [organization-defined measure] for this defect check is above [the organization-defined threshold], then defects in **developing and documenting an inventory of system components which is accurate, complete, detailed, and has specified information** related to this control item might be the cause of the defect, i.e., … absence of required software.
CM-8(a){1}	SWAM-Q01	Non-reporting of device-level SWAM information	a device failing to report within the specified time frame.
CM-8(a){1}	SWAM-Q02	Non-reporting of defect checks	specific defect checks failing to report.
CM-8(a){1}	SWAM-Q03	Low completeness-metric	completeness of overall ISCM reporting not meeting the threshold.

Determination Statement 2

Determination Statement ID	Determination Statement Text
CM-8(a){2}	Determine if the organization: develops and documents an inventory of system components {for software} that is at the level of granularity deemed necessary for tracking and reporting [by the organization].

Roles and Assessment Methods

Determination Statement ID	Implemented By	Assessment Boundary	Assessment Responsibility	Assessment Methods	Selected	Rationale for Risk Acceptance	Frequency of Assessment	Impact of Not Implementing
CM-8(a){2}	ISCM-Sys	ISCM-TN	ISCM-Sys	Test				

Defect Check Rationale Table

A failure in effectiveness of this control item results in a defect in one or more of the following defect checks:

Determination Statement ID	Defect Check ID	Defect Check Name	Rationale
			If an [organization-defined measure] for this defect check is above [the organization-defined threshold], then defects in **developing and documenting the inventory of system components {software} at the level of granularity deemed necessary by the organization for tracking and reporting** related to this control item might be the cause of the defect, i.e., ….
CM-8(a){2}	SWAM-L11	Required software not present	absence of required software.
CM-8(a){2}	SWAM-Q01	Non-reporting of device-level SWAM information	a device failing to report within the specified time frame.
CM-8(a){2}	SWAM-Q02	Non-reporting of defect checks	specific defect checks failing to report.
CM-8(a){2}	SWAM-Q03	Low completeness-metric	completeness of overall ISCM reporting not meeting the threshold.

3.3.3.6 Control Item CM-8(b): INFORMATION SYSTEM COMPONENT INVENTORY

Control Item Text

Control: The organization:

b. Reviews and updates the information system component inventory [Assignment: organization-defined frequency].

Determination Statement 1

Determination Statement ID	Determination Statement Text
CM-8(b){1}	Determine if the organization: updates the system component inventory {for software} [Assignment: organization-defined frequency].

Roles and Assessment Methods

Determination Statement ID	Implemented By	Assessment Boundary	Assessment Responsibility	Assessment Methods	Selected	Rationale for Risk Acceptance	Frequency of Assessment	Impact of Not Implementing
CM-8(b){1}	ISCM-Sys	ISCM-TN	ISCM-Sys	Test				

Defect Check Rationale Table

A failure in effectiveness of this control item results in a defect in one or more of the following defect checks:

Determination Statement ID	Defect Check ID	Defect Check Name	Rationale: If an [organization-defined measure] for this defect check is above [the organization-defined threshold], then defects in updating the system {installed software} component inventory with the organization-defined frequency related to this control item might be the cause of the defect, i.e., ….
CM-8(b){1}	SWAM-L11	Required software not present	absence of required software.
CM-8(b){1}	SWAM-Q04	Poor timeliness metric	poor timeliness of overall ISCM reporting.

Determination Statement 2

Determination Statement ID	Determination Statement Text
CM-8(b){2}	Determine if the organization: reviews the system component inventory {for software} [Assignment: organization-defined frequency].

Roles and Assessment Methods

Determination Statement ID	Implemented By	Assessment Boundary	Assessment Responsibility	Assessment Methods	Selected	Rationale for Risk Acceptance	Frequency of Assessment	Impact of Not Implementing
CM-8(b){2}	DSM	ISCM-TN	ISCM-Sys	Test				

Defect Check Rationale Table

A failure in effectiveness of this control item results in a defect in one or more of the following defect checks:

Determination Statement ID	Defect Check ID	Defect Check Name	Rationale
			If an [organization-defined measure] for this defect check is above [the organization-defined threshold], then defects in **reviewing the system component {software} inventory with the organization-defined frequency** related to this control item might be the cause of the defect, i.e., …
CM-8(b){2}	SWAM-L11	Required software not present	absence of required software.
CM-8(b){2}	SWAM-Q04	Poor timeliness metric	poor timeliness of overall ISCM reporting.

3.3.3.7 Control Item CM-10(a): SOFTWARE USAGE RESTRICTIONS

Control Item Text

Control: The organization:

a. Uses software and associated documentation in accordance with contract agreements and copyright laws.

Determination Statement 1

Determination Statement ID	Determination Statement Text
CM-10(a){1}	Determine if the organization: uses software and associated documentation in accordance with contract agreements and copyright laws.

Roles and Assessment Methods

Determination Statement ID	Implemented By	Assessment Boundary	Assessment Responsibility	Assessment Methods	Selected	Rationale for Risk Acceptance	Frequency of Assessment	Impact of Not Implementing
CM-10(a){1}	DSM	ISCM-TN	ISCM-Sys	Test				

Defect Check Rationale Table

A failure in effectiveness of this control item results in a defect in one or more of the following defect checks:

Determination Statement ID	Defect Check ID	Defect Check Name	Rationale
CM-10(a){1}	SWAM-L10	Unlicensed software	If an [organization-defined measure] for this defect check is above [the organization-defined threshold], then defects in **using software and associated documentation in accordance with contract agreements and copyright laws** related to this control item might be the cause of the defect, i.e., … use of software not in compliance with quantity licenses, contract agreements, or copyright laws.

3.3.3.8 Control Item CM-10(b): SOFTWARE USAGE RESTRICTIONS

Control Item Text

Control: The organization:

b. Tracks the use of software and associated documentation protected by quantity licenses to control copying and distribution.

Determination Statement 1

Determination Statement ID	Determination Statement Text
CM-10(b){1}	Determine if the organization: tracks the use of software protected by quantity licenses to control copying and distribution.

Roles and Assessment Methods

Determination Statement ID	Implemented By	Assessment Boundary	Assessment Responsibility	Assessment Methods	Selected	Rationale for Risk Acceptance	Frequency of Assessment	Impact of Not Implementing
CM-10(b){1}	ISCM-Sys	ISCM-TN	ISCM-Sys	Test				

Defect Check Rationale Table

A failure in effectiveness of this control item results in a defect in one or more of the following defect checks:

Determination Statement ID	Defect Check ID	Defect Check Name	Rationale
CM-10(b){1}	SWAM-L10	Unlicensed software	If an [organization-defined measure] for this defect check is above [the organization-defined threshold], then defects in **tracking the use of software protected by quantity licenses to control copying and distribution** related to this control item might be the cause of the defect, i.e., ... use of software not in compliance with quantity licenses, contract agreements, or copyright laws.

Determination Statement 2

Determination Statement ID	Determination Statement Text
CM-10(b){2}	Determine if the organization: tracks the use of software associated documentation protected by quantity licenses to control copying and distribution.

Roles and Assessment Methods

Determination Statement ID	Implemented By	Assessment Boundary	Assessment Responsibility	Assessment Methods	Selected	Rationale for Risk Acceptance	Frequency of Assessment	Impact of Not Implementing
CM-10(b){2}	DSM	ISCM-TN	MAN	TBD				

Defect Check Rationale Table

A failure in effectiveness of this control item results in a defect in one or more of the following defect checks:

Not applicable because tested manually.

3.3.3.9 Control Item CM-10(c): SOFTWARE USAGE RESTRICTIONS

Control Item Text

Control: The organization:

c. Controls and documents the use of peer-to-peer file sharing technology to ensure that this capability is not used for the unauthorized distribution, display, performance, or reproduction of copyrighted work.

Determination Statement 1

Determination Statement ID	Determination Statement Text
CM-10(c){1}	Determine if the organization: controls and documents the use of peer-to-peer file sharing technology to ensure that this capability is not used for the unauthorized distribution, display, performance, or reproduction of copyrighted work.

Roles and Assessment Methods

Determination Statement ID	Implemented By	Assessment Boundary	Assessment Responsibility	Assessment Methods	Selected	Rationale for Risk Acceptance	Frequency of Assessment	Impact of Not Implementing
CM-10(c){1}	ISCM-Ops	ISCM-TN	ISCM-Sys	Test				

Defect Check Rationale Table

A failure in effectiveness of this control item results in a defect in one or more of the following defect checks:

Determination Statement ID	Defect Check ID	Defect Check Name	Rationale
CM-10(c){1}	SWAM-L10	Unlicensed software	If an [organization-defined measure] for this defect check is above [the organization-defined threshold], then defects in **controlling and documenting the use of peer-to-peer file sharing technology** related to this control item might be the cause of the defect, i.e., …. use of software not in compliance with quantity licenses, contract agreements, or copyright laws.

3.3.3.10 Control Item CM-11(a): USER-INSTALLED SOFTWARE

Control Item Text

Control: The organization:

a. Establishes [Assignment: organization-defined policies] governing the installation of software by users.

Determination Statement 1

Determination Statement ID	Determination Statement Text
CM-11(a){1}	Determine if the organization: establishes [Assignment: organization-defined policies] governing the installation of software by users.

Roles and Assessment Methods

Determination Statement ID	Implemented By	Assessment Boundary	Assessment Responsibility	Assessment Methods	Selected	Rationale for Risk Acceptance	Frequency of Assessment	Impact of Not Implementing
CM-11(a){1}	RskEx	ISCM-TN	ISCM-Sys	Test				

Defect Check Rationale Table

A failure in effectiveness of this control item results in a defect in one or more of the following defect checks:

Determination Statement ID	Defect Check ID	Defect Check Name	Rationale
CM-11(a){1}	SWAM-F02	Unauthorized software installer	If an [organization-defined measure] for this defect check is above [the organization-defined threshold], then defects in **establishing policies governing the installation of software by users** related to this control item might be the cause of the defect, i.e., … the execution of software not installed by an authorized installer.

3.3.3.11 Control Item CM-11(b): USER-INSTALLED SOFTWARE

Control Item Text

Control: The organization:

b. Enforces software installation policies through [Assignment: organization-defined methods].

Determination Statement 1

Determination Statement ID	Determination Statement Text
CM-11(b){1}	Determine if the organization: enforces software installation policies through [Assignment: organization-defined methods].

Roles and Assessment Methods

Determination Statement ID	Implemented By	Assessment Boundary	Assessment Responsibility	Assessment Methods	Selected	Rationale for Risk Acceptance	Frequency of Assessment	Impact of Not Implementing
CM-11(b){1}	ISCM-Ops	ISCM-TN	ISCM-Sys	Test				

Defect Check Rationale Table

A failure in effectiveness of this control item results in a defect in one or more of the following defect checks:

Determination Statement ID	Defect Check ID	Defect Check Name	Rationale If an [organization-defined measure] for this defect check is above [the organization-defined threshold], then defects in **enforcing software installation policies through specified methods** related to this control item might be the cause of the defect, i.e., …
CM-11(b){1}	SWAM-F01	Unauthorized software executes	the execution of unauthorized software.
CM-11(b){1}	SWAM-F02	Unauthorized software installer	the execution of software not installed by an authorized installer.
CM-11(b){1}	SWAM-F03	Unauthorized software directory/folder location	the execution of software not loaded from an approved directory/folder location.
CM-11(b){1}	SWAM-F04	Untrusted core software	lack of core software integrity at start-up.
CM-11(b){1}	SWAM-L04	Devices moving in/out of protective boundaries not in policy compliance	devices' software not being adequately strengthened and/or sanitized for movement into or out of protective boundaries.
CM-11(b){1}	SWAM-L09	Device-software-item assignment to authorization boundary is not 1:1	unclear management responsibility that could lead to unmanaged components.
CM-11(b){1}	SWAM-L10	Unlicensed software	use of software not in compliance with quantity licenses, contract agreements, or copyright laws.
CM-11(b){1}	SWAM-L12	Unmanaged software	the presence of unmanaged software.
CM-11(b){1}	SWAM-L13	Software without warranty and/or source code	the presence of software without warranty and/or source code.

3.3.3.12 Control Item CM-11(c): USER-INSTALLED SOFTWARE

Control Item Text

Control: The organization:

c. Monitors policy compliance at [Assignment: organization-defined frequency].

Determination Statement 1

Determination Statement ID	Determination Statement Text
CM-11(c){1}	Determine if the organization: monitors policy compliance for {installed software} at [Assignment: organization-defined frequency].

Roles and Assessment Methods

Determination Statement ID	Implemented By	Assessment Boundary	Assessment Responsibility	Assessment Methods	Selected	Rationale for Risk Acceptance	Frequency of Assessment	Impact of Not Implementing
CM-11(c){1}	ISCM-Ops	ISCM-TN	ISCM-Sys	Test				

Defect Check Rationale Table

A failure in effectiveness of this control item results in a defect in one or more of the following defect checks:

Determination Statement ID	Defect Check ID	Defect Check Name	Rationale
CM-11(c){1}	SWAM-Q04	Poor timeliness metric	If an [organization-defined measure] for this defect check is above [the organization-defined threshold], then defects in **monitoring policy compliance for {installed software} at the specified frequency** related to this control item might be the cause of the defect, i.e., …. poor timeliness of overall ISCM reporting.

3.3.3.13 Control Item MP-6(a): MEDIA SANITIZATION

Control Item Text

Control: The organization:

a. Sanitizes [Assignment: organization-defined information system media] prior to disposal, release out of organizational control, or release for reuse using [Assignment: organization-defined sanitization techniques and procedures] in accordance with applicable federal and organizational standards and policies.

Determination Statement 1

Determination Statement ID	Determination Statement Text
MP-6(a){1}	Determine if the organization: sanitizes {to remove software} [Assignment: organization-defined information system media] prior to disposal, release out of organizational control, or release for reuse using [Assignment: organization-defined sanitization techniques and procedures] in accordance with applicable federal and organizational standards and policies.

Roles and Assessment Methods

Determination Statement ID	Implemented By	Assessment Boundary	Assessment Responsibility	Assessment Methods	Selected	Rationale for Risk Acceptance	Frequency of Assessment	Impact of Not Implementing
MP-6(a){1}	SWMan	ISCM-TN	ISCM-Sys	Test				

Defect Check Rationale Table

A failure in effectiveness of this control item results in a defect in one or more of the following defect checks:

Determination Statement ID	Defect Check ID	Defect Check Name	Rationale
MP-6(a){1}	SWAM-L04	Devices moving in/out of protective boundaries not in policy compliance	If an [organization-defined measure] for this defect check is above [the organization-defined threshold], then defects in sanitizing {to remove software} media before moving to high risk areas, as required, using approved methods related to this control item might be the cause of the defect, i.e., … : devices' software not being adequately strengthened and/or sanitized for movement into or out of protective boundaries.

3.3.3.14 Control Item MP-6(b): MEDIA SANITIZATION

Control Item Text

Control: The organization:

b. Employs sanitization mechanisms with the strength and integrity commensurate with the security category or classification of the information.

Determination Statement 1

Determination Statement ID	Determination Statement Text
MP-6(b){1}	Determine if the organization: employs sanitization mechanisms {to remove software} with the strength and integrity commensurate with the security category or classification of the information.

Roles and Assessment Methods

Determination Statement ID	Implemented By	Assessment Boundary	Assessment Responsibility	Assessment Methods	Selected	Rationale for Risk Acceptance	Frequency of Assessment	Impact of Not Implementing
MP-6(b){1}	SWMan	ISCM-TN	ISCM-Sys	Test				

Defect Check Rationale Table

A failure in effectiveness of this control item results in a defect in one or more of the following defect checks:

Determination Statement ID	Defect Check ID	Defect Check Name	Rationale
MP-6(b){1}	SWAM-L04	Devices moving in/out of protective boundaries not in policy compliance	If an [organization-defined measure] for this defect check is above [the organization-defined threshold], then defects in **employing sanitization mechanisms {to remove software} with the strength and integrity commensurate with the security category or classification of the information** related to this control item might be the cause of the defect, i.e., ...: devices' software not being adequately strengthened and/or sanitized for movement into or out of protective boundaries.

3.3.3.15 Control Item PS-4(d): PERSONNEL TERMINATION

Control Item Text

Control: The organization, upon termination of individual employment:

d. Retrieves all security-related organizational information system-related property.

Determination Statement 1

Determination Statement ID	Determination Statement Text
PS-4(d){1}	Determine if the organization: retrieves all security-related organizational system-related {software and software media} property.

Roles and Assessment Methods

Determination Statement ID	Implemented By	Assessment Boundary	Assessment Responsibility	Assessment Methods	Selected	Rationale for Risk Acceptance	Frequency of Assessment	Impact of Not Implementing
PS-4(d){1}	SWMan	ISCM-TN	ISCM-Sys	Test				

Defect Check Rationale Table

A failure in effectiveness of this control item results in a defect in one or more of the following defect checks:

Determination Statement ID	Defect Check ID	Defect Check Name	Rationale
PS-4(d){1}	SWAM-L04	Devices moving in/out of protective boundaries not in policy compliance	If an [organization-defined measure] for this defect check is above [the organization-defined threshold], then defects in **retrieving all security-related organizational system-related {software and software media} property** related to this control item might be the cause of the defect, i.e., …. devices' software not being adequately strengthened and/or sanitized for movement into or out of protective boundaries.

3.3.3.16 Control Item SI-3(a): MALICIOUS CODE PROTECTION

Control Item Text

Control: The organization:

a. Employs malicious code protection mechanisms at information system entry and exit points to detect and eradicate malicious code.

Determination Statement 1

Determination Statement ID	Determination Statement Text
SI-3(a){1}	Determine if the organization: employs malicious code protection mechanisms at system entry and exit points to detect and eradicate malicious code.

Roles and Assessment Methods

Determination Statement ID	Implemented By	Assessment Boundary	Assessment Responsibility	Assessment Methods	Selected	Rationale for Risk Acceptance	Frequency of Assessment	Impact of Not Implementing
SI-3(a){1}	ISCM-Ops	ISCM-TN	ISCM-Sys	Test				

Defect Check Rationale Table

A failure in effectiveness of this control item results in a defect in one or more of the following defect checks:

Determination Statement ID	Defect Check ID	Defect Check Name	Rationale
			If an [organization-defined threshold], then defects in **employing malicious code protection mechanisms at system entry and exit points to detect and eradicate malicious code** related to this control item might be the cause of the defect, i.e., …
SI-3(a){1}	SWAM-L14	Poor AV protection	absence of methods to block malware.

3.3.3.17 Control Item SI-3(b): MALICIOUS CODE PROTECTION

Control Item Text

Control: The organization:

b. Updates malicious code protection mechanisms whenever new releases are available in accordance with organizational configuration management policy and procedures.

Determination Statement 1

Determination Statement ID	Determination Statement Text
SI-3(b){1}	Determine if the organization: updates malicious code protection mechanisms whenever new releases are available in accordance with organizational configuration management policy and procedures.

Roles and Assessment Methods

Determination Statement ID	Implemented By	Assessment Boundary	Assessment Responsibility	Assessment Methods	Selected	Rationale for Risk Acceptance	Frequency of Assessment	Impact of Not Implementing
SI-3(b){1}	ISCM-Ops	ISCM-TN	ISCM-Sys	Test				

Defect Check Rationale Table

A failure in effectiveness of this control item results in a defect in one or more of the following defect checks:

Determination Statement ID	Defect Check ID	Defect Check Name	Rationale
			If an [organization-defined measure] for this defect check is above [the organization-defined threshold], then defects in **updating malicious code protection mechanisms whenever new releases are available in accordance with organizational configuration management policy and procedures** related to this control item might be the cause of the defect, i.e., …
SI-3(b){1}	SWAM-F01	Unauthorized software executes	the execution of unauthorized software.
SI-3(b){1}	SWAM-F04	Untrusted core software	lack of core software integrity at start-up.
SI-3(b){1}	SWAM-L04	Devices moving in/out of protective boundaries not in policy compliance	devices' software not being adequately strengthened and/or sanitized for movement into or out of protective boundaries.
SI-3(b){1}	SWAM-L14	Poor AV protection	absence of methods to block malware.

3.3.3.18 Control Item SI-3(c): MALICIOUS CODE PROTECTION

Control Item Text

Control: The organization:

c. Configures malicious code protection mechanisms to:

1. Perform periodic scans of the information system [Assignment: organization-defined frequency] and real-time scans of files from external sources at [Selection (one or more); endpoint; network entry/exit points] as the files are downloaded, opened, or executed in accordance with organizational security policy; and

2. [Selection (one or more): block malicious code; quarantine malicious code; send alert to administrator; [Assignment: organization-defined action]] in response to malicious code detection.

Determination Statement 1

Determination Statement ID	Determination Statement Text
SI-3(c){1}	Determine if the organization: configures malicious code protection mechanisms to perform periodic scans of [software and files that might include hidden software] at an [Assignment: organization-defined frequency] on [devices].

Roles and Assessment Methods

Determination Statement ID	Implemented By	Assessment Boundary	Assessment Responsibility	Assessment Methods	Selected	Rationale for Risk Acceptance	Frequency of Assessment	Impact of Not Implementing
SI-3(c){1}	ISCM-Ops	ISCM-TN	ISCM-Sys	Test				

Defect Check Rationale Table

A failure in effectiveness of this control item results in a defect in one or more of the following defect checks:

Determination Statement ID	Defect Check ID	Defect Check Name	Rationale
SI-3(c){1}	SWAM-L14	Poor AV protection	If an [organization-defined threshold], then defects in **configuring malicious code protection mechanisms to perform periodic scans of {software and files} on mass storage, as specified** related to this control item might be the cause of the defect, i.e., … absence of methods to block malware.

Determination Statement 2

Determination Statement ID	Determination Statement Text
SI-3(c){2}	Determine if the organization: configures malicious code protection mechanisms to perform scans of software and files that might include hidden software at network entry/exit points as the files are downloaded.

Roles and Assessment Methods

Determination Statement ID	Implemented By	Assessment Boundary	Assessment Responsibility	Assessment Methods	Selected	Rationale for Risk Acceptance	Frequency of Assessment	Impact of Not Implementing
SI-3(c){2}	ISCM-Ops	ISCM-TN	ISCM-Sys	Test				

Defect Check Rationale Table

A failure in effectiveness of this control item results in a defect in one or more of the following defect checks:

Determination Statement ID	Defect Check ID	Defect Check Name	Rationale
SI-3(c){2}	SWAM-L14	Poor AV protection	If an [organization-defined measure] for this defect check is above [the organization-defined threshold], then defects in **configuring malicious code protection mechanisms to perform periodic scans of {software and files} at entry and exit points** related to this control item might be the cause of the defect, i.e., … absence of methods to block malware.

Determination Statement 3

Determination Statement ID	Determination Statement Text
SI-3(c){3}	Determine if the organization: configures malicious code protection mechanisms to perform scans of [software and files that might include hidden software] when opened or executed.

Roles and Assessment Methods

Determination Statement ID	Implemented By	Assessment Boundary	Assessment Responsibility	Assessment Methods	Selected	Rationale for Risk Acceptance	Frequency of Assessment	Impact of Not Implementing
SI-3(c){3}	ISCM-Ops	ISCM-TN	ISCM-Sys	Test				

Defect Check Rationale Table

A failure in effectiveness of this control item results in a defect in one or more of the following defect checks:

Determination Statement ID	Defect Check ID	Defect Check Name	Rationale
			If an [organization-defined measure] for this defect check is above [the organization-defined threshold], then defects in **configuring malicious code protection mechanisms to perform periodic scans of {software and files} when opened or executed** related to this control item might be the cause of the defect, i.e., …
SI-3(c){3}	SWAM-F01	Unauthorized software executes	the execution of unauthorized software.
SI-3(c){3}	SWAM-L14	Poor AV protection	absence of methods to block malware.

Determination Statement 4

Determination Statement ID	Determination Statement Text
SI-3(c){4}	Determine if the organization: configures malicious code protection mechanisms to take one or more of the following action(s) when malicious software is detected: [Selection (one or more): block malicious code; quarantine malicious code; send alert to administrator].

Roles and Assessment Methods

Determination Statement ID	Implemented By	Assessment Boundary	Assessment Responsibility	Assessment Methods	Selected	Rationale for Risk Acceptance	Frequency of Assessment	Impact of Not Implementing
SI-3(c){4}	ISCM-Ops	ISCM-TN	ISCM-Sys	Test				

Defect Check Rationale Table

A failure in effectiveness of this control item results in a defect in one or more of the following defect checks:

Determination Statement ID	Defect Check ID	Defect Check Name	Rationale
			If an [organization-defined measure] for this defect check is above [the organization-defined threshold], then defects in **configuring malicious code protection mechanisms to take specific protective actions when malicious software is detected** related to this control item might be the cause of the defect, i.e., …
SI-3(c){4}	SWAM-F01	Unauthorized software executes	the execution of unauthorized software.
SI-3(c){4}	SWAM-L14	Poor AV protection	absence of methods to block malware.

3.3.3.19 Control Item SI-3(d): MALICIOUS CODE PROTECTION

Control Item Text

Control: The organization:

d. Addresses the receipt of false positives during malicious code detection and eradication and the resulting potential impact on the availability of the information system.

Determination Statement 1

Determination Statement ID	Determination Statement Text
SI-3(d){1}	Determine if the organization: addresses the receipt of false positives during malicious code detection and eradication and the resulting potential impact on the availability of the system.

Roles and Assessment Methods

Determination Statement ID	Implemented By	Assessment Boundary	Assessment Responsibility	Assessment Methods	Selected	Rationale for Risk Acceptance	Frequency of Assessment	Impact of Not Implementing
SI-3(d){1}	ISCM-Ops	ISCM-TN	ISCM-Sys	Test				

Defect Check Rationale Table

A failure in effectiveness of this control item results in a defect in one or more of the following defect checks:

Determination Statement ID	Defect Check ID	Defect Check Name	Rationale
			If an [organization-defined measure] for this defect check is above [the organization-defined threshold], then defects in addressing the receipt of false positives during malicious code detection and eradication and the resulting potential impact on the availability of the system related to this control item might be the cause of the defect, i.e, ...
SI-3(d){1}	SWAM-L03	Expired actions on software authorization/deauthorization requests	requested changes not being addressed in a timely manner.

3.3.4 Moderate Baseline Security Control Item Narratives

3.3.4.1 Control Item CM-2(1)(a): BASELINE CONFIGURATION | REVIEWS AND UPDATES

Control Item Text

The organization reviews and updates the baseline configuration of the information system:

(a) [Assignment: organization-defined frequency].

Determination Statement 1

Determination Statement ID	Determination Statement Text
CM-2(1)(a){1}	Determine if the organization: reviews and updates the baseline configuration of the information system: (a) [Assignment: organization-defined frequency].

Roles and Assessment Methods

Determination Statement ID	Implemented By	Assessment Boundary	Assessment Responsibility	Assessment Methods	Selected	Rationale for Risk Acceptance	Frequency of Assessment	Impact of Not Implementing
CM-2(1)(a){1}	DSM	ISCM-TN	ISCM-Sys	Test				

Defect Check Rationale Table

A failure in effectiveness of this control item results in a defect in one or more of the following defect checks:

Determination Statement ID	Defect Check ID	Defect Check Name	Rationale If an [organization-defined measure] for this defect check is above [the organization-defined threshold], then defects in **reviewing and updating the baseline configuration of the information system: [assignment: organization-defined frequency]** related to this control item might be the cause of the defect, i.e., ….
CM-2(1)(a){1}	SWAM-L11	Required software not present	absence of required software.

3.3.4.2 Control Item CM-2(1)(b): BASELINE CONFIGURATION | REVIEWS AND UPDATES

Control Item Text

The organization reviews and updates the baseline configuration of the information system:

(b) When required due to [Assignment organization-defined circumstances].

Determination Statement 1

Determination Statement ID	Determination Statement Text
CM-2(1)(b){1}	Determine if the organization: reviews and updates the baseline configuration of the information system: (b) When required due to [Assignment organization-defined circumstances].

Roles and Assessment Methods

Determination Statement ID	Implemented By	Assessment Boundary	Assessment Responsibility	Assessment Methods	Selected	Rationale for Risk Acceptance	Frequency of Assessment	Impact of Not Implementing
CM-2(1)(b){1}	DSM	ISCM-TN	ISCM-Sys	Test				

Defect Check Rationale Table

A failure in effectiveness of this control item results in a defect in one or more of the following defect checks:

Determination Statement ID	Defect Check ID	Defect Check Name	Rationale
CM-2(1)(b){1}	SWAM-L11	Required software not present	If an [organization-defined measure] for this defect check is above [the organization-defined threshold], then defects in **reviewing and updating the baseline configuration of the information system when required due to [Assignment organization-defined circumstances]** related to this control item might be the cause of the defect, i.e., … : absence of required software.

3.3.4.3 Control Item CM-2(1)(c): BASELINE CONFIGURATION | REVIEWS AND UPDATES

Control Item Text

The organization reviews and updates the baseline configuration of the information system:

(c) As an integral part of information system component installations and upgrades.

Determination Statement 1

Determination Statement ID	Determination Statement Text
CM-2(1)(c){1}	Determine if the organization: reviews and updates the baseline configuration of the information system: (c) As an integral part of information system component installations and upgrades.

Roles and Assessment Methods

Determination Statement ID	Implemented By	Assessment Boundary	Assessment Responsibility	Assessment Methods	Selected	Rationale for Risk Acceptance	Frequency of Assessment	Impact of Not Implementing
CM-2(1)(c){1}	DSM	ISCM-TN	ISCM-Sys	Test				

Defect Check Rationale Table

A failure in effectiveness of this control item results in a defect in one or more of the following defect checks:

Determination Statement ID	Defect Check ID	Defect Check Name	Rationale
CM-2(1)(c){1}	SWAM-L11	Required software not present	If an [organization-defined measure] for this defect check is above [the organization-defined threshold], then defects in reviewing and updating the baseline configuration of the information system as an integral part of information system component installations and upgrades related to this control item might be the cause of the defect, i.e., …: absence of required software.

3.3.4.4 Control Item CM-2(3): BASELINE CONFIGURATION | RETENTION OF PREVIOUS CONFIGURATIONS

Control Item Text

The organization retains [Assignment: organization-defined previous versions of baseline configurations of the information system] to support rollback.

Determination Statement 1

Determination Statement ID	Determination Statement Text
CM-2(3){1}	Determine if the organization: retains [Assignment: organization-defined previous versions of baseline configurations of the information system] to support rollback.

Roles and Assessment Methods

Determination Statement ID	Implemented By	Assessment Boundary	Assessment Responsibility	Assessment Methods	Selected	Rationale for Risk Acceptance	Frequency of Assessment	Impact of Not Implementing
CM-2(3){1}	SWMan	ISCM-TN	ISCM-Sys	Test				

Defect Check Rationale Table

A failure in effectiveness of this control item results in a defect in one or more of the following defect checks:

Determination Statement ID	Defect Check ID	Defect Check Name	Rationale
CM-2(3){1}	SWAM-L05	Number of prior versions of installed software inadequate	If an [organization-defined measure] for this defect check is above [the organization-defined threshold], then defects in **maintaining an adequate number of prior software baseline versions to support rollback** related to this control item might be the cause of the defect, i.e., … lack of prior versions of installed software to enable rollback and recovery.

3.3.4.5 Control Item CM-2(7)(a): BASELINE CONFIGURATION | CONFIGURE SYSTEMS, COMPONENTS, OR DEVICES FOR HIGH-RISK AREAS

Control Item Text

The organization:

(a) Issues [Assignment: organization-defined information systems, system components, or devices] with [Assignment: organization-defined configurations] to individuals traveling to locations that the organization deems to be of significant risk.

Determination Statement 1

Determination Statement ID	Determination Statement Text
CM-2(7)(a){1}	Determine if the organization: issues [Assignment: organization-defined information systems, system components, or devices] with [Assignment: organization-defined configurations] to individuals traveling to locations that the organization deems to be of significant risk.

Roles and Assessment Methods

Determination Statement ID	Implemented By	Assessment Boundary	Assessment Responsibility	Assessment Methods	Selected	Rationale for Risk Acceptance	Frequency of Assessment	Impact of Not Implementing
CM-2(7)(a){1}	SWMan	ISCM-TN	ISCM-Sys	Test				

Defect Check Rationale Table

A failure in effectiveness of this control item results in a defect in one or more of the following defect checks:

Determination Statement ID	Defect Check ID	Defect Check Name	Rationale
CM-2(7)(a){1}	SWAM-L04	Devices moving in/out of protective boundaries not in policy compliance	If an [organization-defined measure] for this defect check is above [the organization-defined threshold], then defects in **issuing [Assignment: organization-defined information systems, system components, or devices] with [Assignment: organization-defined configurations] to individuals traveling to locations that the organization deems to be of significant risk** related to this control item might be the cause of the defect, i.e., … devices' software not being adequately strengthened and/or sanitized for movement into or out of protective boundaries.

3.3.4.6 Control Item CM-2(7)(b): BASELINE CONFIGURATION | CONFIGURE SYSTEMS, COMPONENTS, OR DEVICES FOR HIGH-RISK AREAS

Control Item Text

The organization:

(b) Applies [Assignment: organization-defined security safeguards] to the devices when the individuals return.

Determination Statement 1

Determination Statement ID	Determination Statement Text
CM-2(7)(b){1}	Determine if the organization: applies [Assignment: organization-defined security safeguards] to the devices when the individuals return.

Roles and Assessment Methods

Determination Statement ID	Implemented By	Assessment Boundary	Assessment Responsibility	Assessment Methods	Selected	Rationale for Risk Acceptance	Frequency of Assessment	Impact of Not Implementing
CM-2(7)(b){1}	SWMan	ISCM-TN	ISCM-Sys	Test				

Defect Check Rationale Table

A failure in effectiveness of this control item results in a defect in one or more of the following defect checks:

Determination Statement ID	Defect Check ID	Defect Check Name	Rationale
CM-2(7)(b){1}	SWAM-L04	Devices moving in/out of protective boundaries not in policy compliance	If an [organization-defined measure] for this defect check is above [the organization-defined threshold], then defects in applying [Assignment: organization-defined security safeguards] to the devices when the individuals return related to this control item might be the cause of the defect, i.e., …. devices' software not being adequately strengthened and/or sanitized for movement into or out of protective boundaries.

3.3.4.7 Control Item CM-7(1)(a): LEAST FUNCTIONALITY | PERIODIC REVIEW

Control Item Text

The organization:

(a) Reviews the information system [Assignment: organization-defined frequency] to identify unnecessary and/or nonsecure functions, ports, protocols, and services.

Determination Statement 1

Determination Statement ID	Determination Statement Text
CM-7(1)(a){1}	Determine if the organization: reviews the system {installed software} [Assignment: organization-defined frequency] to identify unnecessary and/or nonsecure functions and services.

Roles and Assessment Methods

Determination Statement ID	Implemented By	Assessment Boundary	Assessment Responsibility	Assessment Methods	Selected	Rationale for Risk Acceptance	Frequency of Assessment	Impact of Not Implementing
CM-7(1)(a){1}	ISCM-Ops	ISCM-TN	ISCM-Sys	Test				

Defect Check Rationale Table

A failure in effectiveness of this control item results in a defect in one or more of the following defect checks:

Determination Statement ID	Defect Check ID	Defect Check Name	Rationale
			If an [organization-defined measure] for this defect check is above [the organization-defined threshold], then defects in **reviewing the system {installed software} often enough to identify unnecessary and/or nonsecure functions and services** related to this control item might be the cause of the defect, i.e., …
CM-7(1)(a){1}	SWAM-L07	Business need of software not recently verified	the presence of software without a recently verified need, resulting in an increase in the attack surface without associated organizational value.
CM-7(1)(a){1}	SWAM-L08	Unused software present	the presence of unneeded software, resulting in an increase in the attack surface.

3.3.4.8 Control Item CM-7(1)(b): LEAST FUNCTIONALITY | PERIODIC REVIEW

Control Item Text

The organization:

(b) Disables [Assignment: organization-defined functions, ports, protocols, and services within the information system deemed to be unnecessary and/or nonsecure].

Determination Statement 1

Determination Statement ID	Determination Statement Text
CM-7(1)(b){1}	Determine if the organization: disables [Assignment: organization-defined {installed software} functions and services within the system deemed to be unnecessary and/or nonsecure].

Roles and Assessment Methods

Determination Statement ID	Implemented By	Assessment Boundary	Assessment Responsibility	Assessment Methods	Selected	Rationale for Risk Acceptance	Frequency of Assessment	Impact of Not Implementing
CM-7(1)(b){1}	DSM	ISCM-TN	ISCM-Sys	Test				

Defect Check Rationale Table

A failure in effectiveness of this control item results in a defect in one or more of the following defect checks:

Determination Statement ID	Defect Check ID	Defect Check Name	Rationale If an [organization-defined measure] for this defect check is above [the organization-defined threshold], then defects in **disabling specified functions and services within the system deemed to be unnecessary and/or nonsecure** related to this control item might be the cause of the defect, i.e., …
CM-7(1)(b){1}	SWAM-F01	Unauthorized software executes	the execution of unauthorized software.
CM-7(1)(b){1}	SWAM-F02	Unauthorized software installer	the execution of software not installed by an authorized installer.
CM-7(1)(b){1}	SWAM-F03	Unauthorized software directory/folder location	the execution of software not loaded from an approved directory/folder location.
CM-7(1)(b){1}	SWAM-F04	Untrusted core software	lack of core software integrity at start-up.
CM-7(1)(b){1}	SWAM-L04	Devices moving in/out of protective boundaries not in policy compliance	devices' software not being adequately strengthened and/or sanitized for movement into or out of protective boundaries.

3.3.4.9 Control Item CM-7(2): LEAST FUNCTIONALITY | PREVENT PROGRAM EXECUTION

Control Item Text

The information system prevents program execution in accordance with [Selection (one or more): [Assignment: organization-defined policies regarding software program usage and restrictions]; rules authorizing the terms and conditions of software program usage].

Determination Statement 1

Determination Statement ID	Determination Statement Text
CM-7(2){1}	Determine if the organization: prevents {installed software} program execution in accordance with [Selection (one or more): [Assignment: organization-defined policies regarding software program usage and restrictions]; rules authorizing the terms and conditions of software program usage].

Roles and Assessment Methods

Determination Statement ID	Implemented By	Assessment Boundary	Assessment Responsibility	Assessment Methods	Selected	Rationale for Risk Acceptance	Frequency of Assessment	Impact of Not Implementing
CM-7(2){1}	ISCM-Ops	ISCM-TN	ISCM-Sys	Test				

Defect Check Rationale Table

A failure in effectiveness of this control item results in a defect in one or more of the following defect checks:

Determination Statement ID	Defect Check ID	Defect Check Name	Rationale If an [organization-defined measure] for this defect check is above [the organization-defined threshold], then defects in **preventing {installed software} program execution as specified** related to this control item might be the cause of the defect, i.e., ...
CM-7(2){1}	SWAM-F01	Unauthorized software executes	the execution of unauthorized software.
CM-7(2){1}	SWAM-F02	Unauthorized software installer	the execution of software not installed by an authorized installer.
CM-7(2){1}	SWAM-F03	Unauthorized software directory/folder location	the execution of software not loaded from an approved directory/folder location.

3.3.4.10 Control Item CM-7(4)(a): LEAST FUNCTIONALITY | UNAUTHORIZED SOFTWARE / BLACKLISTING

Control Item Text

The organization:

(a) Identifies [Assignment: organization-defined software programs not authorized to execute on the information system].

Determination Statement 1

Determination Statement ID	Determination Statement Text
CM-7(4)(a){1}	Determine if the organization: identifies [Assignment: organization-defined software programs not authorized to execute on the system].

Roles and Assessment Methods

Determination Statement ID	Implemented By	Assessment Boundary	Assessment Responsibility	Assessment Methods	Selected	Rationale for Risk Acceptance	Frequency of Assessment	Impact of Not Implementing
CM-7(4)(a){1}	ISCM-Ops	ISCM-TN	ISCM-Sys	Test				

Defect Check Rationale Table

A failure in effectiveness of this control item results in a defect in one or more of the following defect checks:

Determination Statement ID	Defect Check ID	Defect Check Name	Rationale If an [organization-defined measure] for this defect check is above [the organization-defined threshold], then defects in **identifying specified software programs not authorized to execute** related to this control item might be the cause of the defect, i.e., …
CM-7(4)(a){1}	SWAM-F01	Unauthorized software executes	the execution of unauthorized software.
CM-7(4)(a){1}	SWAM-F02	Unauthorized software installer	the execution of software not installed by an authorized installer.
CM-7(4)(a){1}	SWAM-F03	Unauthorized software directory/folder location	the execution of software not loaded from an approved directory/folder location.
CM-7(4)(a){1}	SWAM-F04	Untrusted core software	lack of core software integrity at start-up.
CM-7(4)(a){1}	SWAM-L04	Devices moving in/out of protective boundaries not in policy compliance	devices' software not being adequately strengthened and/or sanitized for movement into or out of protective boundaries.

3.3.4.11 Control Item CM-7(4)(b): LEAST FUNCTIONALITY | UNAUTHORIZED SOFTWARE / BLACKLISTING

Control Item Text

The organization:

(b) Employs an allow-all, deny-by-exception policy to prohibit the execution of unauthorized software programs on the information system.

Determination Statement 1

Determination Statement ID	Determination Statement Text
CM-7(4)(b){1}	Determine if the organization: employs an allow-all, deny-by-exception policy to prohibit the execution of unauthorized software programs on the system.

Roles and Assessment Methods

Determination Statement ID	Implemented By	Assessment Boundary	Assessment Responsibility	Assessment Methods	Selected	Rationale for Risk Acceptance	Frequency of Assessment	Impact of Not Implementing
CM-7(4)(b){1}	RskEx	ISCM-TN	ISCM-Sys	Test				

Defect Check Rationale Table

A failure in effectiveness of this control item results in a defect in one or more of the following defect checks:

Determination Statement ID	Defect Check ID	Defect Check Name	Rationale If an [organization-defined measure] for this defect check is above [the organization-defined threshold], then defects in **employing an allow-all, deny-by-exception policy to prohibit the execution of unauthorized software programs (blacklisting)** related to this control item might be the cause of the defect, i.e., …
CM-7(4)(b){1}	SWAM-F01	Unauthorized software executes	the execution of unauthorized software.
CM-7(4)(b){1}	SWAM-F02	Unauthorized software installer	the execution of software not installed by an authorized installer.
CM-7(4)(b){1}	SWAM-F03	Unauthorized software directory/folder location	the execution of software not loaded from an approved directory/folder location.
CM-7(4)(b){1}	SWAM-F04	Untrusted core software	lack of core software integrity at start-up.
CM-7(4)(b){1}	SWAM-L04	Devices moving in/out of protective boundaries not in policy compliance	devices' software not being adequately strengthened and/or sanitized for movement into or out of protective boundaries.

3.3.4.12 Control Item CM-7(4)(c): LEAST FUNCTIONALITY | UNAUTHORIZED SOFTWARE / BLACKLISTING

Control Item Text

The organization:

(c) Reviews and updates the list of unauthorized software programs [Assignment: organization-defined frequency].

Determination Statement 1

Determination Statement ID	Determination Statement Text
CM-7(4)(c){1}	Determine if the organization: reviews and updates the list of unauthorized software programs [Assignment: organization-defined frequency].

Roles and Assessment Methods

Determination Statement ID	Implemented By	Assessment Boundary	Assessment Responsibility	Assessment Methods	Selected	Rationale for Risk Acceptance	Frequency of Assessment	Impact of Not Implementing
CM-7(4)(c){1}	DSM	ISCM-TN	ISCM-Sys	Test				

Defect Check Rationale Table

A failure in effectiveness of this control item results in a defect in one or more of the following defect checks:

Determination Statement ID	Defect Check ID	Defect Check Name	Rationale
CM-7(4)(c){1}	SWAM-L07	Business need of software not recently verified	If an [organization-defined measure] for this defect check is above [the organization-defined threshold], then defects in **reviewing and updating the list of unauthorized software programs frequently enough** related to this control item might be the cause of the defect, i.e., … the presence of software without a recently verified need, resulting in an increase in the attack surface without associated organizational value.

3.3.4.13 Control Item CM-8(1): INFORMATION SYSTEM COMPONENT INVENTORY | UPDATES DURING INSTALLATIONS / REMOVALS

Control Item Text

The organization updates the inventory of information system components as an integral part of component installations, removals, and information system updates.

Determination Statement 1

Determination Statement ID	Determination Statement Text
CM-8(1){1}	Determine if the organization: updates the inventory of system {installed software} components as an integral part of component installations, removals, and system updates.

Roles and Assessment Methods

Determination Statement ID	Implemented By	Assessment Boundary	Assessment Responsibility	Assessment Methods	Selected	Rationale for Risk Acceptance	Frequency of Assessment	Impact of Not Implementing
CM-8(1){1}	ISCM-Sys	ISCM-TN	ISCM-Sys	Test				

Defect Check Rationale Table

A failure in effectiveness of this control item results in a defect in one or more of the following defect checks:

Determination Statement ID	Defect Check ID	Defect Check Name	Rationale
			If an [organization-defined measure] for this defect check is above [the organization-defined threshold], then defects in **updating the inventory of system {installed software} components as an integral part of component installations, removals, and system updates** related to this control item might be the cause of the defect, i.e., …
CM-8(1){1}	SWAM-L11	Required software not present	absence of required software.
CM-8(1){1}	SWAM-Q04	Poor timeliness metric	poor timeliness of overall ISCM reporting.

3.3.4.14 Control Item CM-8(5): INFORMATION SYSTEM COMPONENT INVENTORY | NO DUPLICATE ACCOUNTING OF COMPONENTS

Control Item Text

The organization verifies that all components within the authorization boundary of the information system are not duplicated in other information system inventories.

Determination Statement 1

Determination Statement ID	Determination Statement Text
CM-8(5){1}	Determine if the organization: verifies that all {installed software} components within the authorization boundary of the system are not duplicated in other system inventories.

Roles and Assessment Methods

Determination Statement ID	Implemented By	Assessment Boundary	Assessment Responsibility	Assessment Methods	Selected	Rationale for Risk Acceptance	Frequency of Assessment	Impact of Not Implementing
CM-8(5){1}	ISCM-Sys	ISCM-TN	ISCM-Sys	Test				

Defect Check Rationale Table

A failure in effectiveness of this control item results in a defect in one or more of the following defect checks:

Determination Statement ID	Defect Check ID	Defect Check Name	Rationale
CM-8(5){1}	SWAM-L09	Device-software-item assignment to authorization boundary is not 1:1	If an [organization-defined measure] for this defect check is above [the organization-defined threshold], then defects in **verifying that all {installed software} components within the authorization boundary of the system are not duplicated in other system inventories** related to this control item might be the cause of the defect, i.e., ... unclear management responsibility that could lead to unmanaged components.

3.3.4.15 Control Item MA-3(1): MAINTENANCE TOOLS | INSPECT TOOLS

Control Item Text

The organization inspects the maintenance tools carried into a facility by maintenance personnel for improper or unauthorized modifications.

Determination Statement 1

Determination Statement ID	Determination Statement Text
MA-3(1){1}	Determine if the organization: inspects the maintenance tools with {installed software} carried into a facility by maintenance personnel for improper or unauthorized modifications to the {installed software}.

Roles and Assessment Methods

Determination Statement ID	Implemented By	Assessment Boundary	Assessment Responsibility	Assessment Methods	Selected	Rationale for Risk Acceptance	Frequency of Assessment	Impact of Not Implementing
MA-3(1){1}	SWMan	ISCM-TN	ISCM-Sys	Test				

Defect Check Rationale Table

A failure in effectiveness of this control item results in a defect in one or more of the following defect checks:

Determination Statement ID	Defect Check ID	Defect Check Name	Rationale
MA-3(1){1}	SWAM-L04	Devices moving in/out of protective boundaries not in policy compliance	If an [organization-defined measure] for this defect check is above [the organization-defined threshold], then defects in inspecting the maintenance tools with {installed software} carried into a facility by maintenance personnel for improper or unauthorized modifications to the {installed software} related to this control item might be the cause of the defect, i.e., ... devices' software not being adequately strengthened and/or sanitized for movement into or out of protective boundaries.

3.3.4.16 Control Item MA-3(2): MAINTENANCE TOOLS | INSPECT MEDIA

Control Item Text

The organization checks media containing diagnostic and test programs for malicious code before the media are used in the information system.

Determination Statement 1

Determination Statement ID	Determination Statement Text
MA-3(2){1}	Determine if the organization: checks media containing diagnostic and test programs for malicious code before the media are used in the system.

Roles and Assessment Methods

Determination Statement ID	Implemented By	Assessment Boundary	Assessment Responsibility	Assessment Methods	Selected	Rationale for Risk Acceptance	Frequency of Assessment	Impact of Not Implementing
MA-3(2){1}	SWMan	ISCM-TN	ISCM-Sys	Test				

Defect Check Rationale Table

A failure in effectiveness of this control item results in a defect in one or more of the following defect checks:

Determination Statement ID	Defect Check ID	Defect Check Name	Rationale
			If an [organization-defined measure] for this defect check is above [the organization-defined threshold], then defects in checking media containing diagnostic and test programs for malicious code before the media are used in the system related to this control item might be the cause of the defect, i.e., ...
MA-3(2){1}	SWAM-F01	Unauthorized software executes	the execution of unauthorized software.
MA-3(2){1}	SWAM-L04	Devices moving in/out of protective boundaries not in policy compliance	devices' software not being adequately strengthened and/or sanitized for movement into or out of protective boundaries.

3.3.4.17 Control Item SC-18(a): MOBILE CODE

Control Item Text

Control: The organization:

a. Defines acceptable and unacceptable mobile code and mobile code technologies.

Determination Statement 1

Determination Statement ID	Determination Statement Text
SC-18(a){1}	Determine if the organization: defines acceptable and unacceptable mobile code and mobile code technologies.

Roles and Assessment Methods

Determination Statement ID	Implemented By	Assessment Boundary	Assessment Responsibility	Assessment Methods	Selected	Rationale for Risk Acceptance	Frequency of Assessment	Impact of Not Implementing
SC-18(a){1}	DSM	ISCM-TN	ISCM-Sys	Test				

Defect Check Rationale Table

A failure in effectiveness of this control item results in a defect in one or more of the following defect checks:

Determination Statement ID	Defect Check ID	Defect Check Name	Rationale
SC-18(a){1}	SWAM-F01	Unauthorized software executes	If an [organization-defined measure] for this defect check is above [the organization-defined threshold], then defects in **defining acceptable and unacceptable mobile code and mobile code technologies** related to this control item might be the cause of the defect, i.e., the execution of unauthorized software.

139

3.3.4.18 Control Item SC-18(b): MOBILE CODE

Control Item Text

Control: The organization:

b. Establishes usage restrictions and implementation guidance for acceptable mobile code and mobile code technologies.

Determination Statement 1

Determination Statement ID	Determination Statement Text
SC-18(b){1}	Determine if the organization: establishes usage restrictions and implementation guidance for acceptable mobile code and mobile code technologies.

Roles and Assessment Methods

Determination Statement ID	Implemented By	Assessment Boundary	Assessment Responsibility	Assessment Methods	Selected	Rationale for Risk Acceptance	Frequency of Assessment	Impact of Not Implementing
SC-18(b){1}	DSM	ISCM-TN	ISCM-Sys	Test				

Defect Check Rationale Table

A failure in effectiveness of this control item results in a defect in one or more of the following defect checks:

Determination Statement ID	Defect Check ID	Defect Check Name	Rationale	
SC-18(b){1}	SWAM-F01	Unauthorized software executes	If an [organization-defined measure] for this defect check is above [the organization-defined threshold], then defects in **establishing usage restrictions and implementation guidance for acceptable mobile code and mobile code technologies** related to this control item might be the cause of the defect, i.e., ...	the execution of unauthorized software.

3.3.4.19 Control Item SC-18(c): MOBILE CODE

Control Item Text

Control: The organization:

     c. Authorizes, monitors, and controls the use of mobile code within the information system.

Determination Statement 1

Determination Statement ID	Determination Statement Text
SC-18(c){1}	Determine if the organization: authorizes, monitors, and controls the use of mobile code within the system.

Roles and Assessment Methods

Determination Statement ID	Implemented By	Assessment Boundary	Assessment Responsibility	Assessment Methods	Selected	Rationale for Risk Acceptance	Frequency of Assessment	Impact of Not Implementing
SC-18(c){1}	ISCM-Ops	ISCM-TN	ISCM-Sys	Test				

Defect Check Rationale Table

A failure in effectiveness of this control item results in a defect in one or more of the following defect checks:

Determination Statement ID	Defect Check ID	Defect Check Name	Rationale	
SC-18(c){1}	SWAM-F01	Unauthorized software executes	If an [organization-defined measure] for this defect check is above [the organization-defined threshold], then defects in **authorizing, monitoring, and controlling the use of mobile code within the system** related to this control item might be the cause of the defect, i.e., …	the execution of unauthorized software.

3.3.4.20 Control Item SI-3(1): MALICIOUS CODE PROTECTION | CENTRAL MANAGEMENT

Control Item Text

The organization centrally manages malicious code protection mechanisms.

Determination Statement 1

Determination Statement ID	Determination Statement Text
SI-3(1){1}	Determine if the organization: centrally manages malicious code protection mechanisms.

Roles and Assessment Methods

Determination Statement ID	Implemented By	Assessment Boundary	Assessment Responsibility	Assessment Methods	Selected	Rationale for Risk Acceptance	Frequency of Assessment	Impact of Not Implementing
SI-3(1){1}	ISCM-Ops	ISCM-TN	ISCM-Sys	Test				

Defect Check Rationale Table

A failure in effectiveness of this control item results in a defect in one or more of the following defect checks:

Determination Statement ID	Defect Check ID	Defect Check Name	Rationale
SI-3(1){1}	SWAM-F02	Unauthorized software installer	If an [organization-defined measure] for this defect check is above [the organization-defined threshold], then defects in **centrally managing malicious code protection mechanisms** related to this control item might be the cause of the defect, i.e., …. the execution of software not installed by an authorized installer.

3.3.4.21 Control Item SI-3(2): MALICIOUS CODE PROTECTION | AUTOMATIC UPDATES

Control Item Text

The information system automatically updates malicious code protection mechanisms.

Determination Statement 1

Determination Statement ID	Determination Statement Text
SI-3(2){1}	Determine if the organization: automatically updates malicious code protection mechanisms.

Roles and Assessment Methods

Determination Statement ID	Implemented By	Assessment Boundary	Assessment Responsibility	Assessment Methods	Selected	Rationale for Risk Acceptance	Frequency of Assessment	Impact of Not Implementing
SI-3(2){1}	ISCM-Ops	ISCM-TN	ISCM-Sys	Test				

Defect Check Rationale Table

A failure in effectiveness of this control item results in a defect in one or more of the following defect checks:

Determination Statement ID	Defect Check ID	Defect Check Name	Rationale
SI-3(2){1}	SWAM-L03	Expired actions on software authorization/deauthorization requests	If an [organization-defined measure] for this defect check is above [the organization-defined threshold], then defects in **automatically updating malicious code protection mechanisms** related to this control item might be the cause of the defect, i.e., …. requested changes not being addressed in a timely manner.

3.3.4.22 Control Item SI-7: SOFTWARE, FIRMWARE, AND INFORMATION INTEGRITY

Control Item Text

Control: The organization employs integrity verification tools to detect unauthorized changes to [Assignment: organization-defined software, firmware, and information].

Determination Statement 1

Determination Statement ID	Determination Statement Text
SI-7{1}	Determine if the organization: employs integrity verification tools to detect unauthorized changes to [Assignment: an organization-defined subset of software, firmware, and information].

Roles and Assessment Methods

Determination Statement ID	Implemented By	Assessment Boundary	Assessment Responsibility	Assessment Methods	Selected	Rationale for Risk Acceptance	Frequency of Assessment	Impact of Not Implementing
SI-7{1}	ISCM-Ops	ISCM-TN	ISCM-Sys	Test				

Defect Check Rationale Table

A failure in effectiveness of this control item results in a defect in one or more of the following defect checks:

Determination Statement ID	Defect Check ID	Defect Check Name	Rationale
			If an [organization-defined measure] for this defect check is above [the organization-defined threshold], then defects in **employing integrity verification tools to detect unauthorized changes to specified software** related to this control item might be the cause of the defect, i.e., …
SI-7{1}	SWAM-F01	Unauthorized software executes	the execution of unauthorized software.
SI-7{1}	SWAM-L01	Unapproved authorizer	lack of verification that software was authorized by approved accounts (persons).
SI-7{1}	SWAM-L02	Required authorizations missing	careless or malicious authorization of software.

3.3.4.23 Control Item SI-7(1): SOFTWARE, FIRMWARE, AND INFORMATION INTEGRITY | INTEGRITY CHECKS

Control Item Text

The information system performs an integrity check of [Assignment: organization-defined software, firmware, and information] [Selection (one or more): at startup; at [Assignment: organization-defined transitional states or security-relevant events]; [Assignment: organization-defined frequency]].

Determination Statement 1

Determination Statement ID	Determination Statement Text
SI-7(1){1}	Determine if the organization: performs an integrity check of [Assignment: organization-defined software, firmware, and information] [Selection (one or more): at startup; at [Assignment: organization-defined transitional states or security-relevant events]; [Assignment: organization-defined frequency]].

Roles and Assessment Methods

Determination Statement ID	Implemented By	Assessment Boundary	Assessment Responsibility	Assessment Methods	Selected	Rationale for Risk Acceptance	Frequency of Assessment	Impact of Not Implementing
SI-7(1){1}	ISCM-Ops	ISCM-TN	ISCM-Sys	Test				

Defect Check Rationale Table

A failure in effectiveness of this control item results in a defect in one or more of the following defect checks:

Determination Statement ID	Defect Check ID	Defect Check Name	Rationale
SI-7(1){1}	SWAM-F04	Untrusted core software	If an [organization-defined measure] for this defect check is above [the organization-defined threshold], then defects in **performing an integrity check of specified software at specified times** related to this control item might be the cause of the defect, i.e., … lack of core software integrity at start-up.

3.3.4.24 Control Item SI-16: MEMORY PROTECTION

Control Item Text

Control: The information system implements [Assignment: organization-defined security safeguards] to protect its memory from unauthorized code execution.

Determination Statement 1

Determination Statement ID	Determination Statement Text
SI-16{1}	Determine if the organization: implements [Assignment: organization-defined security safeguards] to protect its memory from unauthorized code execution.

Roles and Assessment Methods

Determination Statement ID	Implemented By	Assessment Boundary	Assessment Responsibility	Assessment Methods	Selected	Rationale for Risk Acceptance	Frequency of Assessment	Impact of Not Implementing
SI-16{1}	TBD	ISCM-TN	MAN	TBD				

Defect Check Rationale Table

A failure in effectiveness of this control item results in a defect in one or more of the following defect checks:

Not applicable because tested manually.

3.3.5 High Baseline Security Control Item Narratives

3.3.5.1 Control Item CM-3(1)(c): CONFIGURATION CHANGE CONTROL | AUTOMATED DOCUMENT / NOTIFICATION / PROHIBITION OF CHANGES

Control Item Text

The organization employs automated mechanisms to:

(c) Highlight proposed changes to the information system that have not been approved or disapproved by [Assignment: organization-defined time period].

Determination Statement 1

Determination Statement ID	Determination Statement Text
CM-3(1)(c){1}	Determine if the organization: employs automated mechanisms to highlight proposed changes to the system {installed software} that have not been approved or disapproved by [Assignment: organization-defined time period].

Roles and Assessment Methods

Determination Statement ID	Implemented By	Assessment Boundary	Assessment Responsibility	Assessment Methods	Selected	Rationale for Risk Acceptance	Frequency of Assessment	Impact of Not Implementing
CM-3(1)(c){1}	ISCM-Sys	ISCM-TN	ISCM-Sys	Test				

Defect Check Rationale Table

A failure in effectiveness of this control item results in a defect in one or more of the following defect checks:

Determination Statement ID	Defect Check ID	Defect Check Name	Rationale
CM-3(1)(c){1}	SWAM-L03	Expired actions on software authorization/deauthorization requests	If an [organization-defined measure] for this defect check is above [the organization-defined threshold], then defects in **employing automated mechanisms to highlight proposed changes to the system {installed software} that have not been approved or disapproved by [Assignment: organization-defined time period]** related to this control item might be the cause of the defect, i.e., ... requested changes not being addressed in a timely manner.

3.3.5.2 Control Item CM-4: SECURITY IMPACT ANALYSIS | SEPARATE TEST ENVIRONMENTS

Control Item Text

The organization analyzes changes to the information system in a separate test environment before implementation in an operational environment, looking for security impacts due to flaws, weaknesses, incompatibility, or intentional malice.

Determination Statement 1

Determination Statement ID	Determination Statement Text
CM-4(1){1}	Determine if the organization: analyzes changes to the information system {software} in a separate test environment before implementation in an operational environment, looking for security impacts due to flaws, weaknesses, incompatibility, or intentional malice.

Roles and Assessment Methods

Determination Statement ID	Implemented By	Assessment Boundary	Assessment Responsibility	Assessment Methods	Selected	Rationale for Risk Acceptance	Frequency of Assessment	Impact of Not Implementing
CM-4(1){1}	DSM	ISCM-TN	ISCM-Sys	Test				

Defect Check Rationale Table

A failure in effectiveness of this control item results in a defect in one or more of the following defect checks:

Determination Statement ID	Defect Check ID	Defect Check Name	Rationale
CM-4(1){1}	SWAM-L06	Testing and validation of software inadequate	If an [organization-defined measure] for this defect check is above [the organization-defined threshold], then defects in analyzing changes to the information system {software}, looking for security impacts due to flaws, weaknesses, incompatibility, or intentional malice related to this control item might be the cause of the defect, i.e., … lack of adequate testing and validation.

3.3.5.3 Control Item CM-5(3): ACCESS RESTRICTIONS FOR CHANGE | SIGNED COMPONENTS

Control Item Text

The information system prevents the installation of [Assignment: organization-defined software and firmware components] without verification that the component has been digitally signed using a certificate that is recognized and approved by the organization.

Determination Statement 1

Determination Statement ID	Determination Statement Text
CM-5(3){1}	Determine if the organization: verifies that the {software} component has been digitally signed using a certificate that is recognized and approved by the organization before installation of [Assignment: organization-defined software and firmware components].

Roles and Assessment Methods

Determination Statement ID	Implemented By	Assessment Boundary	Assessment Responsibility	Assessment Methods	Selected	Rationale for Risk Acceptance	Frequency of Assessment	Impact of Not Implementing
CM-5(3){1}	SWMan	ISCM-TN	ISCM-Sys	Test				

Defect Check Rationale Table

A failure in effectiveness of this control item results in a defect in one or more of the following defect checks:

Determination Statement ID	Defect Check ID	Defect Check Name	Rationale
			If an [organization-defined measure] for this defect check is above [the organization-defined threshold], then defects in **verifying that the {software} component has been digitally signed using a certificate that is recognized and approved by the organization before installation of specific components** related to this control item might be the cause of the defect, i.e., …
CM-5(3){1}	SWAM-F01	Unauthorized software executes	the execution of unauthorized software.
CM-5(3){1}	SWAM-F04	Untrusted core software	lack of core software integrity at start-up.

3.3.5.4 Control Item CM-7(5)(a): LEAST FUNCTIONALITY | AUTHORIZED SOFTWARE / WHITELISTING

Control Item Text

The organization:

(a) Identifies [Assignment: organization-defined software programs authorized to execute on the information system].

Determination Statement 1

Determination Statement ID	Determination Statement Text
CM-7(5)(a){1}	Determine if the organization: identifies [Assignment: organization-defined software programs authorized to execute on the system].

Roles and Assessment Methods

Determination Statement ID	Implemented By	Assessment Boundary	Assessment Responsibility	Assessment Methods	Selected	Rationale for Risk Acceptance	Frequency of Assessment	Impact of Not Implementing
CM-7(5)(a){1}	DSM	ISCM-TN	ISCM-Sys	Test				

Defect Check Rationale Table

A failure in effectiveness of this control item results in a defect in one or more of the following defect checks:

Determination Statement ID	Defect Check ID	Defect Check Name	Rationale If an [organization-defined measure] for this defect check is above [the organization-defined threshold], then defects in **identifying specific software programs authorized to execute on the system** related to this control item might be the cause of the defect, i.e., ...
CM-7(5)(a){1}	SWAM-F01	Unauthorized software executes	the execution of unauthorized software.
CM-7(5)(a){1}	SWAM-F02	Unauthorized software installer	the execution of software not installed by an authorized installer.
CM-7(5)(a){1}	SWAM-F03	Unauthorized software directory/folder location	the execution of software not loaded from an approved directory/folder location.
CM-7(5)(a){1}	SWAM-F04	Untrusted core software	lack of core software integrity at start-up.
CM-7(5)(a){1}	SWAM-L04	Devices moving in/out of protective boundaries not in policy compliance	devices' software not being adequately strengthened and/or sanitized for movement into or out of protective boundaries.

3.3.5.5 Control Item CM-7(5)(b): LEAST FUNCTIONALITY | AUTHORIZED SOFTWARE / WHITELISTING

Control Item Text

The organization:

(b) Employs a deny-all, permit-by-exception policy to allow the execution of authorized software programs on the information system.

Determination Statement 1

Determination Statement ID	Determination Statement Text
CM-7(5)(b){1}	Determine if the organization: employs a deny-all, permit-by-exception policy to allow the execution of authorized software programs on the system.

Roles and Assessment Methods

Determination Statement ID	Implemented By	Assessment Boundary	Assessment Responsibility	Assessment Methods	Selected	Rationale for Risk Acceptance	Frequency of Assessment	Impact of Not Implementing
CM-7(5)(b){1}	RskEx	ISCM-TN	ISCM-Sys	Test				

Defect Check Rationale Table

A failure in effectiveness of this control item results in a defect in one or more of the following defect checks:

Determination Statement ID	Defect Check ID	Defect Check Name	Rationale If an [organization-defined measure] for this defect check is above [the organization-defined threshold], then defects in **employing a deny-all, permit-by-exception policy to allow the execution of authorized software programs (whitelisting)** related to this control item might be the cause of the defect, i.e., …
CM-7(5)(b){1}	SWAM-F01	Unauthorized software executes	the execution of unauthorized software.
CM-7(5)(b){1}	SWAM-F02	Unauthorized software installer	the execution of software not installed by an authorized installer.
CM-7(5)(b){1}	SWAM-F03	Unauthorized software directory/folder location	the execution of software not loaded from an approved directory/folder location.
CM-7(5)(b){1}	SWAM-F04	Untrusted core software	lack of core software integrity at start-up.
CM-7(5)(b){1}	SWAM-L04	Devices moving in/out of protective boundaries not in policy compliance	devices' software not being adequately strengthened and/or sanitized for movement into or out of protective boundaries.

3.3.5.6 Control Item CM-7(5)(c): LEAST FUNCTIONALITY | AUTHORIZED SOFTWARE / WHITELISTING

Control Item Text

The organization:

(c) Reviews and updates the list of authorized software programs [Assignment: organization-defined frequency].

Determination Statement 1

Determination Statement ID	Determination Statement Text
CM-7(5)(c){1}	Determine if the organization: reviews and updates the list of authorized software programs [Assignment: organization-defined frequency].

Roles and Assessment Methods

Determination Statement ID	Implemented By	Assessment Boundary	Assessment Responsibility	Assessment Methods	Selected	Rationale for Risk Acceptance	Frequency of Assessment	Impact of Not Implementing
CM-7(5)(c){1}	DSM	ISCM-TN	ISCM-Sys	Test				

Defect Check Rationale Table

A failure in effectiveness of this control item results in a defect in one or more of the following defect checks:

Determination Statement ID	Defect Check ID	Defect Check Name	Rationale
			If an [organization-defined measure] for this defect check is above [the organization-defined threshold], then defects in **reviewing and updating the list of authorized software programs at the required frequency** related to this control item might be the cause of the defect, i.e., ····
CM-7(5)(c){1}	SWAM-L07	Business need of software not recently verified	the presence of software without a recently verified need, resulting in an increase in the attack surface without associated organizational value.

3.3.5.7 Control Item CM-8(4): INFORMATION SYSTEM COMPONENT INVENTORY | ACCOUNTABILITY INFORMATION

Control Item Text

The organization includes in the information system component inventory information, a means for identifying by [Selection (one or more): name; position; role], individuals responsible/accountable for administering those components.

Determination Statement 1

Determination Statement ID	Determination Statement Text
CM-8(4){1}	Determine if the organization: includes in the {installed software} system component inventory information, a means for identifying by [Selection (one or more): name; position; role], individuals responsible/accountable for administering those components.

Roles and Assessment Methods

Determination Statement ID	Implemented By	Assessment Boundary	Assessment Responsibility	Assessment Methods	Selected	Rationale for Risk Acceptance	Frequency of Assessment	Impact of Not Implementing
CM-8(4){1}	DSM	ISCM-TN	ISCM-Sys	Test				

Defect Check Rationale Table

A failure in effectiveness of this control item results in a defect in one or more of the following defect checks:

Determination Statement ID	Defect Check ID	Defect Check Name	Rationale
			If an [organization-defined measure] for this defect check is above [the organization-defined threshold], then defects in including in the {installed software} system component inventory information a means for identifying individuals responsible or accountable for administering those components related to this control item might be the cause of the defect, i.e., …
CM-8(4){1}	SWAM-L12	Unmanaged software	the presence of unmanaged software.

3.3.5.8 Control Item MP-6(1): MEDIA SANITIZATION | REVIEW / APPROVE / TRACK / DOCUMENT / VERIFY

Control Item Text

The organization reviews, approves, tracks, documents, and verifies media sanitization and disposal actions.

Determination Statement 1

Determination Statement ID	Determination Statement Text
MP-6(1){1}	Determine if the organization: reviews, approves, tracks, documents, and verifies media sanitization and disposal actions {to remove software}.

Roles and Assessment Methods

Determination Statement ID	Implemented By	Assessment Boundary	Assessment Responsibility	Assessment Methods	Selected	Rationale for Risk Acceptance	Frequency of Assessment	Impact of Not Implementing
MP-6(1){1}	SWMan	ISCM-TN	ISCM-Sys	Test				

Defect Check Rationale Table

A failure in effectiveness of this control item results in a defect in one or more of the following defect checks:

Determination Statement ID	Defect Check ID	Defect Check Name	Rationale
MP-6(1){1}	SWAM-L04	Devices moving in/out of protective boundaries not in policy compliance	If an [organization-defined measure] for this defect check is above [the organization-defined threshold], then defects in **reviewing, approving, tracking, documenting, and verifying media sanitization and disposal actions {to remove software}** related to this control item might be the cause of the defect, i.e., ... devices' software not being adequately strengthened and/or sanitized for movement into or out of protective boundaries.

3.3.5.9 Control Item MP-6(2): MEDIA SANITIZATION | EQUIPMENT TESTING

Control Item Text

The organization tests sanitization equipment and procedures [Assignment: organization-defined frequency] to verify that the intended sanitization is being achieved.

Determination Statement 1

Determination Statement ID	Determination Statement Text
MP-6(2){1}	Determine if the organization: tests sanitization equipment and procedures [Assignment: organization-defined frequency] to verify that the intended sanitization {to remove software} is being achieved.

Roles and Assessment Methods

Determination Statement ID	Implemented By	Assessment Boundary	Assessment Responsibility	Assessment Methods	Selected	Rationale for Risk Acceptance	Frequency of Assessment	Impact of Not Implementing
MP-6(2){1}	SWMan	ISCM-TN	ISCM-Sys	Test				

Defect Check Rationale Table

A failure in effectiveness of this control item results in a defect in one or more of the following defect checks:

Determination Statement ID	Defect Check ID	Defect Check Name	Rationale
MP-6(2){1}	SWAM-L04	Devices moving in/out of protective boundaries not in policy compliance	If an [organization-defined measure] for this defect check is above [the organization-defined threshold], then defects in testing sanitization equipment and procedures [Assignment: organization-defined frequency] to verify that the intended sanitization {to remove software} is being achieved related to this control item might be the cause of the defect, i.e., ... devices' software not being adequately strengthened and/or sanitized for movement into or out of protective boundaries.

3.3.5.10 Control Item MP-6(3): MEDIA SANITIZATION | NONDESTRUCTIVE TECHNIQUES

Control Item Text

The organization applies nondestructive sanitization techniques to portable storage devices prior to connecting such devices to the information system under the following circumstances: [Assignment: organization-defined circumstances requiring sanitization of portable storage devices].

Determination Statement 1

Determination Statement ID	Determination Statement Text
MP-6(3){1}	Determine if the organization: applies nondestructive sanitization techniques {to remove software} to portable storage devices prior to connecting such devices to the information system under the following circumstances: [Assignment: organization-defined circumstances requiring sanitization of portable storage devices].

Roles and Assessment Methods

Determination Statement ID	Implemented By	Assessment Boundary	Assessment Responsibility	Assessment Methods	Selected	Rationale for Risk Acceptance	Frequency of Assessment	Impact of Not Implementing
MP-6(3){1}	SWMan	ISCM-TN	ISCM-Sys	Test				

Defect Check Rationale Table

A failure in effectiveness of this control item results in a defect in one or more of the following defect checks:

Determination Statement ID	Defect Check ID	Defect Check Name	Rationale
MP-6(3){1}	SWAM-L04	Devices moving in/out of protective boundaries not in policy compliance	If an [organization-defined measure] for this defect check is above [the organization-defined threshold], then defects in applying nondestructive sanitization techniques {to remove software} to portable storage devices prior to connecting such devices to the information system when moved from high risk areas related to this control item might be the cause of the defect, i.e., ... devices' software not being adequately strengthened and/or sanitized for movement into or out of protective boundaries.

3.3.5.11 Control Item SA-12: SUPPLY CHAIN PROTECTION

Control Item Text

Control: The organization protects against supply chain threats to the information system, system component, or information system service by employing [Assignment: organization-defined security safeguards] as part of a comprehensive, defense-in-breadth information security strategy.

Determination Statement 1

Determination Statement ID	Determination Statement Text
SA-12{1}	Determine if the organization: protects against supply chain threats to the system {installed software} by employing [Assignment: organization-defined security safeguards] as part of a comprehensive, defense-in-breadth information security strategy.

Roles and Assessment Methods

Determination Statement ID	Implemented By	Assessment Boundary	Assessment Responsibility	Assessment Methods	Selected	Rationale for Risk Acceptance	Frequency of Assessment	Impact of Not Implementing
SA-12{1}	DSM	ISCM-TN	ISCM-Sys	Test				

Defect Check Rationale Table

A failure in effectiveness of this control item results in a defect in one or more of the following defect checks:

Determination Statement ID	Defect Check ID	Defect Check Name	Rationale	
			If an [organization-defined measure] for this defect check is above [the organization-defined threshold], then defects in **protecting against supply chain threats to the system as specified** related to this control item might be the cause of the defect, i.e., …	
SA-12{1}	SWAM-F01	Unauthorized software executes	the execution of unauthorized software.	

3.3.5.12 Control Item SI-7(14)(a): SOFTWARE, FIRMWARE, AND INFORMATION INTEGRITY | BINARY OR MACHINE EXECUTABLE CODE

Control Item Text

The organization:

(a) Prohibits the use of binary or machine-executable code from sources with limited or no warranty and without the provision of source code.

Determination Statement 1

Determination Statement ID	Determination Statement Text
SI-7(14)(a){1}	Determine if the organization: prohibits the use of binary or machine-executable code from sources with limited or no warranty and/or without the provision of source code.

Roles and Assessment Methods

Determination Statement ID	Implemented By	Assessment Boundary	Assessment Responsibility	Assessment Methods	Selected	Rationale for Risk Acceptance	Frequency of Assessment	Impact of Not Implementing
SI-7(14)(a){1}	RskEx	ISCM-TN	ISCM-Sys	Test				

Defect Check Rationale Table

A failure in effectiveness of this control item results in a defect in one or more of the following defect checks:

Determination Statement ID	Defect Check ID	Defect Check Name	Rationale	
SI-7(14)(a){1}	SWAM-L13	Software without warranty and/or source code	If an [organization-defined measure] for this defect check is above [the organization-defined threshold], then defects in **prohibiting the use of binary or machine-executable code from sources with limited or no warranty and/or without the provision of source code** related to this control item might be the cause of the defect, i.e., ….	the presence of software without warranty and/or source code.

3.3.5.13 Control Item SI-7(14)(b): SOFTWARE, FIRMWARE, AND INFORMATION INTEGRITY | BINARY OR MACHINE EXECUTABLE CODE

Control Item Text

The organization:

(b) Provides exceptions to the source code requirement only for compelling mission/operational requirements and with the approval of the authorizing official.

Determination Statement 1

Determination Statement ID	Determination Statement Text
SI-7(14)(b){1}	Determine if the organization: provides exceptions to the source code requirement only for compelling mission/operational requirements and with the approval of the authorizing official.

Roles and Assessment Methods

Determination Statement ID	Implemented By	Assessment Boundary	Assessment Responsibility	Assessment Methods	Selected	Rationale for Risk Acceptance	Frequency of Assessment	Impact of Not Implementing
SI-7(14)(b){1}	RskEx	ISCM-TN	ISCM-Sys	Test				

Defect Check Rationale Table

A failure in effectiveness of this control item results in a defect in one or more of the following defect checks:

Determination Statement ID	Defect Check ID	Defect Check Name	Rationale
			If an [organization-defined measure] for this defect check is above [the organization-defined threshold], then defects in **providing exceptions to the source code requirement only for compelling mission/operational requirements and with the approval of the authorizing official** related to this control item might be the cause of the defect, i.e., …
SI-7(14)(b){1}	SWAM-L01	Unapproved authorizer	lack of verification that software was authorized by approved accounts (persons).

3.4 Control Allocation Tables (CATs)

Table 8: Low Baseline Control (Item) Allocation Table, Table 9: Moderate Baseline Control (Item) Allocation Table, and Table 10: High Baseline Control (Item) Allocation Table, provide the low, moderate, and high baseline control allocations, respectively. The following is a summary of the material in the security plan assessment narrative for each determination statement in Section 3.3. It provides a concise summary of the assessment plan.

3.4.1 Low Baseline Control Allocation Table

Table 8: Low Baseline Control (Item) Allocation Table

Determination Statement ID	Implemented By	Assessment Boundary	Assessment Responsibility	Assessment Methods	Selected	Rationale for Risk Acceptance	Frequency of Assessment	Impact of Not Implementing
CM-2{1}	DSM	ISCM-TN	ISCM-Sys	Test				
CM-4{1}	DSM	ISCM-TN	ISCM-Sys	Test				
CM-7(a){1}	DSM	ISCM-TN	ISCM-Sys	Test				
CM-7(b){1}	DSM	ISCM-TN	ISCM-Sys	Test				
CM-8(a){1}	DSM	ISCM-TN	ISCM-Sys	Test				
CM-8(a){2}	ISCM-Sys	ISCM-TN	ISCM-Sys	Test				
CM-8(b){1}	ISCM-Sys	ISCM-TN	ISCM-Sys	Test				
CM-8(b){2}	DSM	ISCM-TN	ISCM-Sys	Test				
CM-10(a){1}	DSM	ISCM-TN	ISCM-Sys	Test				
CM-10(b){1}	ISCM-Sys	ISCM-TN	ISCM-Sys	Test				
CM-10(b){2}	DSM	ISCM-TN	MAN	TBD				
CM-10(c){1}	ISCM-Ops	ISCM-TN	ISCM-Sys	Test				
CM-11(a){1}	RskEx	ISCM-TN	ISCM-Sys	Test				
CM-11(b){1}	ISCM-Ops	ISCM-TN	ISCM-Sys	Test				
CM-11(c){1}	ISCM-Ops	ISCM-TN	ISCM-Sys	Test				
MP-6(a){1}	SWMan	ISCM-TN	ISCM-Sys	Test				
MP-6(b){1}	SWMan	ISCM-TN	ISCM-Sys	Test				
PS-4(d){1}	SWMan	ISCM-TN	ISCM-Sys	Test				
SI-3(a){1}	ISCM-Ops	ISCM-TN	ISCM-Sys	Test				
SI-3(b){1}	ISCM-Ops	ISCM-TN	ISCM-Sys	Test				
SI-3(c){1}	ISCM-Ops	ISCM-TN	ISCM-Sys	Test				
SI-3(c){2}	ISCM-Ops	ISCM-TN	ISCM-Sys	Test				
SI-3(c){3}	ISCM-Ops	ISCM-TN	ISCM-Sys	Test				

Determination Statement ID	Implemented By	Assessment Boundary	Assessment Responsibility	Assessment Methods	Selected	Rationale for Risk Acceptance	Frequency of Assessment	Impact of Not Implementing
SI-3(c){4}	ISCM-Ops	ISCM-TN	ISCM-Sys	Test				
SI-3(d){1}	ISCM-Ops	ISCM-TN	ISCM-Sys	Test				

3.4.2 Moderate Baseline Control Allocation Table

Table 9: Moderate Baseline Control (Item) Allocation Table

Determination Statement ID	Implemented By	Assessment Boundary	Assessment Responsibility	Assessment Methods	Selected	Rationale for Risk Acceptance	Frequency of Assessment	Impact of Not Implementing
CM-2(1)(a){1}	DSM	ISCM-TN	ISCM-Sys	Test				
CM-2(1)(b){1}	DSM	ISCM-TN	ISCM-Sys	Test				
CM-2(1)(c){1}	DSM	ISCM-TN	ISCM-Sys	Test				
CM-2(3){1}	SWMan	ISCM-TN	ISCM-Sys	Test				
CM-2(7)(a){1}	SWMan	ISCM-TN	ISCM-Sys	Test				
CM-2(7)(b){1}	SWMan	ISCM-TN	ISCM-Sys	Test				
CM-7(1)(a){1}	ISCM-Ops	ISCM-TN	ISCM-Sys	Test				
CM-7(1)(b){1}	DSM	ISCM-TN	ISCM-Sys	Test				
CM-7(2){1}	ISCM-Ops	ISCM-TN	ISCM-Sys	Test				
CM-7(4)(a){1}	ISCM-Ops	ISCM-TN	ISCM-Sys	Test				
CM-7(4)(b){1}	RskEx	ISCM-TN	ISCM-Sys	Test				
CM-7(4)(c){1}	DSM	ISCM-TN	ISCM-Sys	Test				
CM-8(1){1}	ISCM-Sys	ISCM-TN	ISCM-Sys	Test				
CM-8(5){1}	ISCM-Sys	ISCM-TN	ISCM-Sys	Test				
MA-3(1){1}	SWMan	ISCM-TN	ISCM-Sys	Test				
MA-3(2){1}	SWMan	ISCM-TN	ISCM-Sys	Test				
SC-18(a){1}	DSM	ISCM-TN	ISCM-Sys	Test				
SC-18(b){1}	DSM	ISCM-TN	ISCM-Sys	Test				
SC-18(c){1}	ISCM-Ops	ISCM-TN	ISCM-Sys	Test				
SI-3(1){1}	ISCM-Ops	ISCM-TN	ISCM-Sys	Test				
SI-3(2){1}	ISCM-Ops	ISCM-TN	ISCM-Sys	Test				
SI-7{1}	ISCM-Ops	ISCM-TN	ISCM-Sys	Test				
SI-7(1){1}	ISCM-Ops	ISCM-TN	ISCM-Sys	Test				
SI-16{1}	TBD	ISCM-TN	MAN	TBD				

3.4.3 High Baseline Control Allocation Table

Table 10: High Baseline Control (Item) Allocation Table

Determination Statement ID	Implemented By	Assessment Boundary	Assessment Responsibility	Assessment Methods	Selected	Rationale for Risk Acceptance	Frequency of Assessment	Impact of Not Implementing
CM-3(1)(c){1}	ISCM-Sys	ISCM-TN	ISCM-Sys	Test				
CM-4(1){1}	DSM	ISCM-TN	ISCM-Sys	Test				
CM-5(3){1}	SWMan	ISCM-TN	ISCM-Sys	Test				
CM-7(5)(a){1}	DSM	ISCM-TN	ISCM-Sys	Test				
CM-7(5)(b){1}	RskEx	ISCM-TN	ISCM-Sys	Test				
CM-7(5)(c){1}	DSM	ISCM-TN	ISCM-Sys	Test				
CM-8(4){1}	DSM	ISCM-TN	ISCM-Sys	Test				
MP-6(1){1}	SWMan	ISCM-TN	ISCM-Sys	Test				
MP-6(2){1}	SWMan	ISCM-TN	ISCM-Sys	Test				
MP-6(3){1}	SWMan	ISCM-TN	ISCM-Sys	Test				
SA-12{1}	DSM	ISCM-TN	ISCM-Sys	Test				
SI-7(14)(a){1}	RskEx	ISCM-TN	ISCM-Sys	Test				
SI-7(14)(b){1}	RskEx	ISCM-TN	ISCM-Sys	Test				

Appendix A. Traceability of SWAM Control I'
Attack Steps

Note: This Appendix includes only those control items that can be
automation.

Example Attack Step	SP 800-53 Con.
1) Gain Internal Entry	CM-2(7)(a)
1) Gain Internal Entry	CM-2(7)(b)
1) Gain Internal Entry	CM-4
1) Gain Internal Entry	CM-4(1)
1) Gain Internal Entry	CM-7(1)(b)
1) Gain Internal Entry	CM-7(4)(a)
1) Gain Internal Entry	CM-7(4)(b)
1) Gain Internal Entry	CM-7(5)(a)
1) Gain Internal Entry	CM-7(5)(b)
1) Gain Internal Entry	CM-8(4)
1) Gain Internal Entry	CM-11(b)
1) Gain Internal Entry	MA-3(1)
1) Gain Internal Entry	MA-3(2)
1) Gain Internal Entry	MP-6(a)
1) Gain Internal Entry	MP-6(b)
1) Gain Internal Entry	MP-6(1)
1) Gain Internal Entry	MP-6(2)
1) Gain Internal Entry	MP-6(3)
1) Gain Internal Entry	PS-4(d)
1) Gain Internal Entry	SI-3(b)
3) Gain Foothold	CM-4
3) Gain Foothold	CM-4(1)
3) Gain Foothold	CM-5(3)
3) Gain Foothold	CM-7(a)
3) Gain Foothold	CM-7(b)
3) Gain Foothold	CM-7(1)(a)
3) Gain Foothold	CM-7(1)(b)
3) Gain Foothold	CM-7(2)
3) Gain Foothold	CM-7(4)(a)
3) Gain Foothold	CM-7(4)(b)
3) Gain Foothold	CM-7(4)(c)
3) Gain Foothold	CM-7(5)(a)
3) Gain Foothold	CM-7(5)(b)
3) Gain Foothold	CM-7(5)(c)

Example Attack Step	SP 800-53 Control Item Code
3) Gain Foothold	CM-11(a)
3) Gain Foothold	CM-11(b)
3) Gain Foothold	MA-3(2)
3) Gain Foothold	SA-12
3) Gain Foothold	SC-18(a)
3) Gain Foothold	SC-18(b)
3) Gain Foothold	SC-18(c)
3) Gain Foothold	SI-3(b)
3) Gain Foothold	SI-3(c)
3) Gain Foothold	SI-3(1)
3) Gain Foothold	SI-7
3) Gain Foothold	SI-7(14)(a)
3) Gain Foothold	SI-7(14)(b)
4) Gain Persistence	CM-3(1)(c)
4) Gain Persistence	CM-4
4) Gain Persistence	CM-5(3)
4) Gain Persistence	CM-7(a)
4) Gain Persistence	CM-7(b)
4) Gain Persistence	CM-7(1)(a)
4) Gain Persistence	CM-7(1)(b)
4) Gain Persistence	CM-7(2)
4) Gain Persistence	CM-7(4)(a)
4) Gain Persistence	CM-7(4)(b)
4) Gain Persistence	CM-7(4)(c)
4) Gain Persistence	CM-7(5)(a)
4) Gain Persistence	CM-7(5)(b)
4) Gain Persistence	CM-7(5)(c)
4) Gain Persistence	CM-8(4)
4) Gain Persistence	CM-8(5)
4) Gain Persistence	CM-10(a)
4) Gain Persistence	CM-10(b)
4) Gain Persistence	CM-10(c)
4) Gain Persistence	CM-11(a)
4) Gain Persistence	CM-11(b)
4) Gain Persistence	SI-3(a)
4) Gain Persistence	SI-3(b)
4) Gain Persistence	SI-3(c)
4) Gain Persistence	SI-3(d)
4) Gain Persistence	SI-3(1)

Example Attack Step	SP 800-53 Control Item Code
4) Gain Persistence	SI-3(2)
4) Gain Persistence	SI-7
4) Gain Persistence	SI-7(1)
4) Gain Persistence	SI-7(14)(a)
4) Gain Persistence	SI-7(14)(b)
6) Achieve Attack Objective	CM-2
6) Achieve Attack Objective	CM-2(1)(a)
6) Achieve Attack Objective	CM-2(1)(b)
6) Achieve Attack Objective	CM-2(1)(c)
6) Achieve Attack Objective	CM-2(3)
6) Achieve Attack Objective	CM-4
6) Achieve Attack Objective	CM-8(a)
6) Achieve Attack Objective	CM-8(b)
6) Achieve Attack Objective	CM-8(1)
6) Achieve Attack Objective	CM-10(a)
6) Achieve Attack Objective	CM-10(b)
6) Achieve Attack Objective	CM-10(c)
6) Achieve Attack Objective	CM-11(b)

Appendix B. Keyword Rules Used to Identify Controls that Support SWAM

Automated keyword searches were employed to identify candidate control items in SP 800-53 that might support the SWAM capability. After candidate controls were returned by the keyword searches, the language content of each control item was examined manually, to separate those that do support the SWAM capability (true positives) from those that do not (false positives). The control items for the low, moderate, and high baselines are listed in Tables, 8, 9, and 10, respectively. The specific keyword rules used to identify SWAM controls appear in the table below.

Keywords to Match in SP 800-53	Rationale
anti-counterfeit	Applies to counterfeit software.
authorized software	The organization authorizes software using either a deny-by-exception or allow-by-exception strategy.
automatic AND *execution*	Reduce the chance that newly inserted unapproved software will execute.
change control	The organization needs a change control process to determine authorized software.
flaw remediation	CVEs and CWEs (whether flaws have been remediated) should be considered when approving software initially and on an ongoing basis.
function isolation	CVEs and CWEs related to function isolation should be considered when approving software initially and on an ongoing basis.
heterogen	Using heterogeneous software is a strategy to make a system less attackable.
high-risk areas	Types and instances of software are more controlled in high risk areas. When returning from a high-risk area, the software is suspect, as it may have been modified.
inventory	The organization must know its current inventory, to compare to the authorized inventory.
least func NOT *software program*	Unneeded software and software functions should be removed or disabled.
malicious code OR *malware*	Reduce the chance that unapproved software will execute.
mobile code	Mobile code requires extra and/or different protections.
non-persisten OR *persisten*	Reduce the chance that unapproved software will execute and/or persist
operating system-independent application OR *platform-independent application*	OS- and platform-independent software is often attacked more frequently as it is present on more devices.
peer-to-peer	Managing peer-to-peer software helps address copyright issues; however, peer-to-peer software may also introduce security vulnerabilities.

Keywords to Match in SP 800-53	Rationale
process isolation	The degree of process isolation present, e.g., whether inter-process communication is allowed, is a consideration when authorizing software.
property	Licensed software needs control as property to avoid licensing violations, which could lead to non-patching and other issues.
supply chain NOT *monitoring*	Only software from an approved supply chain should be authorized (and present)
software AND *restrict*	Only authorized software should be present on the target network
software usage restriction NOT *peer-to-peer*	Only authorized software should be present on the target network
tamper resistance	Only software from an approved supply chain should be authorized (and present) to ensure software integrity and resist tampering.
unsupport AND *system*	Unsupported software becomes increasingly vulnerable.
user AND *software* AND *install*	Only authorized installers should be able to install software.
user AND *software* AND *govern*	A process is needed to authorize and manage installed software.
user AND *software* AND *polic*	Policy is needed to authorize and manage installed software.

Appendix C. Control Items in the Low-High Baseline that were Selected by the Keyword Search for Controls that Support SWAM, but were Manually Determined to be False Positives

SP 800-53 Control Item	Control Text	Level	Rationale for Calling a False Positive
AC-6 (1)	LEAST PRIVILEGE | AUTHORIZE ACCESS TO SECURITY FUNCTIONS The organization explicitly authorizes access to [Assignment: organization-defined security functions (deployed in hardware, software, and firmware) and security-relevant information].	Moderate	Relates to privileges and accounts
SA-11	DEVELOPER SECURITY TESTING AND EVALUATION Control: The organization requires the developer of the information system, system component, or information system service to: d. Implement a verifiable flaw remediation process.	Moderate	Relates to flaw remediation (VULN) rather than software asset management (SWAM)
SC-39	PROCESS ISOLATION Control: The information system maintains a separate execution domain for each executing process.	Low	Relates to separation of processes (internal boundaries - BOUND), rather than to SWAM
SI-2	FLAW REMEDIATION Control: The organization: b. Tests software and firmware updates related to flaw remediation for effectiveness and potential side effects before installation.	Low	Relates to flaw remediation (VULN) rather than to SWAM
SI-2 (1)	FLAW REMEDIATION | CENTRAL MANAGEMENT The organization centrally manages the flaw remediation process.	High	Relates to flaw remediation (VULN) rather than to SWAM
SI-2 (2)	FLAW REMEDIATION | AUTOMATED FLAW REMEDIATION STATUS The organization employs automated mechanisms [Assignment: organization-defined frequency] to determine the state of information system components with regard to flaw remediation.	Moderate	Relates to flaw remediation (VULN) rather than to SWAM
SI-7 (2)	SOFTWARE, FIRMWARE, AND INFORMATION INTEGRITY | AUTOMATED NOTIFICATIONS OF INTEGRITY VIOLATIONS The organization employs automated tools that provide notification to [Assignment: organization-defined personnel or roles] upon discovering discrepancies during integrity verification.	High	Relates to behavioral expectations (BEHAVE) rather than SWAM

SP 800-53 Control Item	Control Text	Level	Rationale for Calling a False Positive
SI-7 (5)	SOFTWARE, FIRMWARE, AND INFORMATION INTEGRITY | AUTOMATED RESPONSE TO INTEGRITY VIOLATIONS The information system automatically [Selection (one or more): shuts the information system down; restarts the information system; implements [Assignment: organization-defined security safeguards]] when integrity violations are discovered.	High	Focus is on detect incidents and contingencies (DETECT) and respond to incidents and contingencies (RESPOND) rather than SWAM
SI-7 (7)	SOFTWARE, FIRMWARE, AND INFORMATION INTEGRITY | INTEGRATION OF DETECTION AND RESPONSE The organization incorporates the detection of unauthorized [Assignment: organization-defined security-relevant changes to the information system] into the organizational incident response capability.	Moderate	Relates to preparation for events (PREPARE) rather than SWAM

Appendix D. Control Items Not in the Low, Moderate, or High Baselines

The following security controls items are not included in an SP 800-53 baseline and thus were not analyzed further after the keyword search:

- the Program Management (PM) Family, because the PM controls do not apply to individual systems;

- control items selected by the SWAM keywords (as specified in Appendix B) but that are not assigned to an SP 800-53 baseline; and

- the Privacy Controls.

The control items matching the criteria in the bulleted list above are provided in this appendix in case an organization wants to develop its own automated tests.

SP 800-53 Control Item	Control Text
AT-3(4)	SECURITY TRAINING	SUSPICIOUS COMMUNICATIONS AND ANOMALOUS SYSTEM BEHAVIOR The organization provides training to its personnel on [Assignment: organization-defined indicators of malicious code] to recognize suspicious communications and anomalous behavior in organizational information systems.
CM-3(3)	CONFIGURATION CHANGE CONTROL	AUTOMATED CHANGE IMPLEMENTATION The organization employs automated mechanisms to implement changes to the current information system baseline and deploys the updated baseline across the installed base.
CM-3(4)	CONFIGURATION CHANGE CONTROL	SECURITY REPRESENTATIVE The organization requires an information security representative to be a member of the [Assignment: organization-defined configuration change control element].
CM-3(5)	CONFIGURATION CHANGE CONTROL	AUTOMATED SECURITY RESPONSE The information system implements [Assignment: organization-defined security responses] automatically if baseline configurations are changed in an unauthorized manner.
CM-3(6)	CONFIGURATION CHANGE CONTROL	CRYPTOGRAPHY MANAGEMENT The organization ensures that cryptographic mechanisms used to provide [Assignment: organization-defined security safeguards] are under configuration management.

SP 800-53 Control Item	Control Text
CM-5(6)	ACCESS RESTRICTIONS FOR CHANGE | LIMIT LIBRARY PRIVILEGES The organization limits privileges to change software resident within software libraries.
CM-7(3)	LEAST FUNCTIONALITY | REGISTRATION COMPLIANCE The organization ensures compliance with [Assignment: organization-defined registration requirements for functions, ports, protocols, and services].
CM-8(6)	INFORMATION SYSTEM COMPONENT INVENTORY | ASSESSED CONFIGURATIONS / APPROVED DEVIATIONS The organization includes assessed component configurations and any approved deviations to current deployed configurations in the information system component inventory.
CM-8(7)	INFORMATION SYSTEM COMPONENT INVENTORY | CENTRALIZED REPOSITORY The organization provides a centralized repository for the inventory of information system components.
CM-8(8)	INFORMATION SYSTEM COMPONENT INVENTORY | AUTOMATED LOCATION TRACKING The organization employs automated mechanisms to support tracking of information system components by geographic location.
CM-8(9)(a)	INFORMATION SYSTEM COMPONENT INVENTORY | ASSIGNMENT OF COMPONENTS TO SYSTEMS The organization: (a) Assigns [Assignment: organization-defined acquired information system components] to an information system.
CM-8(9)(b)	INFORMATION SYSTEM COMPONENT INVENTORY | ASSIGNMENT OF COMPONENTS TO SYSTEMS The organization: (b) Receives an acknowledgement from the information system owner of this assignment.
CM-10(1)	SOFTWARE USAGE RESTRICTIONS | OPEN SOURCE SOFTWARE The organization establishes the following restrictions on the use of open source software: [Assignment: organization-defined restrictions].
CM-11(1)	USER-INSTALLED SOFTWARE | ALERTS FOR UNAUTHORIZED INSTALLATIONS The information system alerts [Assignment: organization-defined personnel or roles] when the unauthorized installation of software is detected.
CM-11(2)	USER-INSTALLED SOFTWARE | PROHIBIT INSTALLATION WITHOUT PRIVILEGED STATUS The information system prohibits user installation of software without explicit privileged status.
CP-10(6)	INFORMATION SYSTEM RECOVERY AND RECONSTITUTION | COMPONENT PROTECTION The organization protects backup and restoration hardware, firmware, and software.

SP 800-53 Control Item	Control Text
IR-4(10)	INCIDENT HANDLING | SUPPLY CHAIN COORDINATION The organization coordinates incident handling activities involving supply chain events with other organizations involved in the supply chain.
IR-6(3)	INCIDENT REPORTING | COORDINATION WITH SUPPLY CHAIN The organization provides security incident information to other organizations involved in the supply chain for information systems or information system components related to the incident.
IR-10	INTEGRATED INFORMATION SECURITY ANALYSIS TEAM Control: The organization establishes an integrated team of forensic/malicious code analysts, tool developers, and real-time operations personnel.
PM-5	INFORMATION SYSTEM INVENTORY Control: The organization develops and maintains an inventory of its information systems.
SA-10(1)	DEVELOPER CONFIGURATION MANAGEMENT | SOFTWARE / FIRMWARE INTEGRITY VERIFICATION The organization requires the developer of the information system, system component, or information system service to enable integrity verification of software and firmware components.
SA-10(4)	DEVELOPER CONFIGURATION MANAGEMENT | TRUSTED GENERATION The organization requires the developer of the information system, system component, or information system service to employ tools for comparing newly generated versions of security-relevant hardware descriptions and software/firmware source and object code with previous versions.
SA-10(5)	DEVELOPER CONFIGURATION MANAGEMENT | MAPPING INTEGRITY FOR VERSION CONTROL The organization requires the developer of the information system, system component, or information system service to maintain the integrity of the mapping between the master build data (hardware drawings and software/firmware code) describing the current version of security-relevant hardware, software, and firmware and the on-site master copy of the data for the current version.
SA-10(6)	DEVELOPER CONFIGURATION MANAGEMENT | TRUSTED DISTRIBUTION The organization requires the developer of the information system, system component, or information system service to execute procedures for ensuring that security-relevant hardware, software, and firmware updates distributed to the organization are exactly as specified by the master copies.
SA-12(1)	SUPPLY CHAIN PROTECTION | ACQUISITION STRATEGIES / TOOLS / METHODS The organization employs [Assignment: organization-defined tailored acquisition strategies, contract tools, and procurement methods] for the purchase of the information system, system component, or information system service from suppliers.

SP 800-53 Control Item	Control Text
SA-12(2)	SUPPLY CHAIN PROTECTION | SUPPLIER REVIEWS The organization conducts a supplier review prior to entering into a contractual agreement to acquire the information system, system component, or information system service
SA-12(5)	SUPPLY CHAIN PROTECTION | LIMITATION OF HARM The organization employs [Assignment: organization-defined security safeguards] to limit harm from potential adversaries identifying and targeting the organizational supply chain.
SA-12(7)	SUPPLY CHAIN PROTECTION | ASSESSMENTS PRIOR TO SELECTION / ACCEPTANCE / UPDATE The organization conducts an assessment of the information system, system component, or information system service prior to selection, acceptance, or update.
SA-12(8)	SUPPLY CHAIN PROTECTION | USE OF ALL-SOURCE INTELLIGENCE The organization uses all-source intelligence analysis of suppliers and potential suppliers of the information system, system component, or information system service.
SA-12(9)	SUPPLY CHAIN PROTECTION | OPERATIONS SECURITY The organization employs [Assignment: organization-defined Operations Security (OPSEC) safeguards] in accordance with classification guides to protect supply chain-related information for the information system, system component, or information system service.
SA-12(10)	SUPPLY CHAIN PROTECTION | VALIDATE AS GENUINE AND NOT ALTERED The organization employs [Assignment: organization-defined security safeguards] to validate that the information system or system component received is genuine and has not been altered.
SA-12(11)	SUPPLY CHAIN PROTECTION | PENETRATION TESTING / ANALYSIS OF ELEMENTS, PROCESSES, AND ACTORS The organization employs [Selection (one or more): organizational analysis, independent third-party analysis, organizational penetration testing, independent third-party penetration testing] of [Assignment: organization-defined supply chain elements, processes, and actors] associated with the information system, system component, or information system service.
SA-12(12)	SUPPLY CHAIN PROTECTION | INTER-ORGANIZATIONAL AGREEMENTS The organization establishes inter-organizational agreements and procedures with entities involved in the supply chain for the information system, system component, or information system service.
SA-12(13)	SUPPLY CHAIN PROTECTION | CRITICAL INFORMATION SYSTEM COMPONENTS The organization employs [Assignment: organization-defined security safeguards] to ensure an adequate supply of [Assignment: organization-defined critical information system components].

SP 800-53 Control Item	Control Text
SA-12(14)	SUPPLY CHAIN PROTECTION | IDENTITY AND TRACEABILITY The organization establishes and retains unique identification of [Assignment: organization-defined supply chain elements, processes, and actors] for the information system, system component, or information system service.
SA-12(15)	SUPPLY CHAIN PROTECTION | PROCESSES TO ADDRESS WEAKNESSES OR DEFICIENCIES The organization establishes a process to address weaknesses or deficiencies in supply chain elements identified during independent or organizational assessments of such elements.
SA-17(2)(a)	DEVELOPER SECURITY ARCHITECTURE AND DESIGN | SECURITY-RELEVANT COMPONENTS The organization requires the developer of the information system, system component, or information system service to: (a) Define security-relevant hardware, software, and firmware.
SA-17(2)(b)	DEVELOPER SECURITY ARCHITECTURE AND DESIGN | SECURITY-RELEVANT COMPONENTS The organization requires the developer of the information system, system component, or information system service to: (b) Provide a rationale that the definition for security-relevant hardware, software, and firmware is complete.
SA-17(3)(a)	DEVELOPER SECURITY ARCHITECTURE AND DESIGN | FORMAL CORRESPONDENCE The organization requires the developer of the information system, system component, or information system service to: (a) Produce, as an integral part of the development process, a formal top-level specification that specifies the interfaces to security-relevant hardware, software, and firmware in terms of exceptions, error messages, and effects.
SA-17(3)(c)	DEVELOPER SECURITY ARCHITECTURE AND DESIGN | FORMAL CORRESPONDENCE The organization requires the developer of the information system, system component, or information system service to: (c) Show via informal demonstration, that the formal top-level specification completely covers the interfaces to security-relevant hardware, software, and firmware.
SA-17(3)(d)	DEVELOPER SECURITY ARCHITECTURE AND DESIGN | FORMAL CORRESPONDENCE The organization requires the developer of the information system, system component, or information system service to: (d) Show that the formal top-level specification is an accurate description of the implemented security-relevant hardware, software, and firmware.

SP 800-53 Control Item	Control Text
SA-17(3)(e)	DEVELOPER SECURITY ARCHITECTURE AND DESIGN | FORMAL CORRESPONDENCE The organization requires the developer of the information system, system component, or information system service to: (e) Describe the security-relevant hardware, software, and firmware mechanisms not addressed in the formal top-level specification but strictly internal to the security-relevant hardware, software, and firmware.
SA-17(4)(a)	DEVELOPER SECURITY ARCHITECTURE AND DESIGN | INFORMAL CORRESPONDENCE The organization requires the developer of the information system, system component, or information system service to: (a) Produce, as an integral part of the development process, an informal descriptive top-level specification that specifies the interfaces to security-relevant hardware, software, and firmware in terms of exceptions, error messages, and effects.
SA-17(4)(c)	DEVELOPER SECURITY ARCHITECTURE AND DESIGN | INFORMAL CORRESPONDENCE The organization requires the developer of the information system, system component, or information system service to: (c) Show via informal demonstration, that the descriptive top-level specification completely covers the interfaces to security-relevant hardware, software, and firmware.
SA-17(4)(d)	DEVELOPER SECURITY ARCHITECTURE AND DESIGN | INFORMAL CORRESPONDENCE The organization requires the developer of the information system, system component, or information system service to: (d) Show that the descriptive top-level specification is an accurate description of the interfaces to security-relevant hardware, software, and firmware.
SA-17(4)(e)	DEVELOPER SECURITY ARCHITECTURE AND DESIGN | INFORMAL CORRESPONDENCE The organization requires the developer of the information system, system component, or information system service to: (e) Describe the security-relevant hardware, software, and firmware mechanisms not addressed in the descriptive top-level specification but strictly internal to the security-relevant hardware, software, and firmware.
SA-17(5)(a)	DEVELOPER SECURITY ARCHITECTURE AND DESIGN | CONCEPTUALLY SIMPLE DESIGN The organization requires the developer of the information system, system component, or information system service to: (a) Design and structure the security-relevant hardware, software, and firmware to use a complete, conceptually simple protection mechanism with precisely defined semantics.

SP 800-53 Control Item	Control Text
SA-17(5)(b)	DEVELOPER SECURITY ARCHITECTURE AND DESIGN | CONCEPTUALLY SIMPLE DESIGN The organization requires the developer of the information system, system component, or information system service to: (b) Internally structure the security-relevant hardware, software, and firmware with specific regard for this mechanism.
SA-17(6)	DEVELOPER SECURITY ARCHITECTURE AND DESIGN | STRUCTURE FOR TESTING The organization requires the developer of the information system, system component, or information system service to structure security-relevant hardware, software, and firmware to facilitate testing.
SA-17(7)	DEVELOPER SECURITY ARCHITECTURE AND DESIGN | STRUCTURE FOR LEAST PRIVILEGE The organization requires the developer of the information system, system component, or information system service to structure security-relevant hardware, software, and firmware to facilitate controlling access with least privilege.
SA-18	TAMPER RESISTANCE AND DETECTION Control: The organization implements a tamper protection program for the information system, system component, or information system service.
SA-18(1)	TAMPER RESISTANCE AND DETECTION | MULTIPLE PHASES OF SDLC The organization employs anti-tamper technologies and techniques during multiple phases in the system development life cycle including design, development, integration, operations, and maintenance.
SA-18(2)	TAMPER RESISTANCE AND DETECTION | INSPECTION OF INFORMATION SYSTEMS, COMPONENTS, OR DEVICES The organization inspects [Assignment: organization-defined information systems, system components, or devices] [Selection (one or more): at random; at [Assignment: organization-defined frequency], upon [Assignment: organization-defined indications of need for inspection]] to detect tampering.
SA-19(a)	COMPONENT AUTHENTICITY Control: The organization: a. Develops and implements anti-counterfeit policy and procedures that include the means to detect and prevent counterfeit components from entering the information system.
SA-19(1)	COMPONENT AUTHENTICITY | ANTI-COUNTERFEIT TRAINING The organization trains [Assignment: organization-defined personnel or roles] to detect counterfeit information system components (including hardware, software, and firmware).
SA-19(4)	COMPONENT AUTHENTICITY | ANTI-COUNTERFEIT TRAINING The organization scans for counterfeit information system components [Assignment: organization-defined frequency].

SP 800-53 Control Item	Control Text
SA-22(a)	UNSUPPORTED SYSTEM COMPONENTS Control: The organization: a. Replaces information system components when support for the components is no longer available from the developer, vendor, or manufacturer.
SA-22(b)	UNSUPPORTED SYSTEM COMPONENTS Control: The organization: b. Provides justification and documents approval for the continued use of unsupported system components required to satisfy mission/business needs.
SA-22(1)	UNSUPPORTED SYSTEM COMPONENTS | ALTERNATIVE SOURCES FOR CONTINUED SUPPORT The organization provides [Selection (one or more): in-house support; [Assignment: organization-defined support from external providers]] for unsupported information system components.
SC-3(1)	SECURITY FUNCTION ISOLATION | HARDWARE SEPARATION The information system utilizes underlying hardware separation mechanisms to implement security function isolation.
SC-3(2)	SECURITY FUNCTION ISOLATION | ACCESS / FLOW CONTROL FUNCTIONS The information system isolates security functions enforcing access and information flow control from nonsecurity functions and from other security functions.
SC-3(3)	SECURITY FUNCTION ISOLATION | MINIMIZE NONSECURITY FUNCTIONALITY The organization minimizes the number of nonsecurity functions included within the isolation boundary containing security functions.
SC-3(4)	SECURITY FUNCTION ISOLATION | MODULE COUPLING AND COHESIVENESS The organization implements security functions as largely independent modules that maximize internal cohesiveness within modules and minimize coupling between modules.
SC-3(5)	SECURITY FUNCTION ISOLATION | LAYERED STRUCTURES The organization implements security functions as a layered structure minimizing interactions between layers of the design and avoiding any dependence by lower layers on the functionality or correctness of higher layers.
SC-18(1)	MOBILE CODE | IDENTIFY UNACCEPTABLE CODE / TAKE CORRECTIVE ACTIONS The information system identifies [Assignment: organization-defined unacceptable mobile code] and takes [Assignment: organization-defined corrective actions].

SP 800-53 Control Item	Control Text
SC-18(2)	MOBILE CODE | ACQUISITION / DEVELOPMENT / USE The organization ensures that the acquisition, development, and use of mobile code to be deployed in the information system meets [Assignment: organization-defined mobile code requirements].
SC-18(3)	MOBILE CODE | PREVENT DOWNLOADING / EXECUTION The information system prevents the download and execution of [Assignment: organization-defined unacceptable mobile code].
SC-18(4)	MOBILE CODE | PREVENT AUTOMATIC EXECUTION The information system prevents the automatic execution of mobile code in [Assignment: organization-defined software applications] and enforces [Assignment: organization-defined actions] prior to executing the code.
SC-18(5)	MOBILE CODE | ALLOW EXECUTION ONLY IN CONFINED ENVIRONMENTS The organization allows execution of permitted mobile code only in confined virtual machine environments.
SC-27	PLATFORM-INDEPENDENT APPLICATIONS Control: The information system includes: [Assignment: organization-defined platform-independent applications].
SC-29	HETEROGENEITY Control: The organization employs a diverse set of information technologies for [Assignment: organization-defined information system components] in the implementation of the information system.
SC-29(1)	HETEROGENEITY | VIRTUALIZATION TECHNIQUES The organization employs virtualization techniques to support the deployment of a diversity of operating systems and applications that are changed [Assignment: organization-defined frequency].
SC-34(1)	NON-MODIFIABLE EXECUTABLE PROGRAMS | NO WRITABLE STORAGE The organization employs [Assignment: organization-defined information system components] with no writeable storage that is persistent across component restart or power on/off.
SC-34(3)(a)	NON-MODIFIABLE EXECUTABLE PROGRAMS | HARDWARE-BASED PROTECTION The organization: (a) Employs hardware-based, write-protect for [Assignment: organization-defined information system firmware components].

SP 800-53 Control Item	Control Text
SC-34(3)(b)	NON-MODIFIABLE EXECUTABLE PROGRAMS | HARDWARE-BASED PROTECTION The organization: (b) Implements specific procedures for [Assignment: organization-defined authorized individuals] to manually disable hardware write-protect for firmware modifications and re-enable the write-protect prior to returning to operational mode.
SC-35	HONEYCLIENTS Control: The information system includes components that proactively seek to identify malicious websites and/or web-based malicious code.
SC-39(1)	PROCESS ISOLATION | HARDWARE SEPARATION The information system implements underlying hardware separation mechanisms to facilitate process separation.
SC-39(2)	PROCESS ISOLATION | THREAD ISOLATION The information system maintains a separate execution domain for each thread in [Assignment: organization-defined multi-threaded processing].
SE-1(a)	INVENTORY OF PERSONALLY IDENTIFIABLE INFORMATION Control: The organization: a. Establishes, maintains, and updates [Assignment: organization-defined frequency] an inventory that contains a listing of all programs and information systems identified as collecting, using, maintaining, or sharing personally identifiable information (PII).
SE-1(b)	INVENTORY OF PERSONALLY IDENTIFIABLE INFORMATION Control: The organization: b. Provides each update of the PII inventory to the CIO or information security official [Assignment: organization-defined frequency] to support the establishment of information security requirements for all new or modified information systems containing PII.
SI-2(3)(a)	FLAW REMEDIATION | TIME TO REMEDIATE FLAWS / BENCHMARKS FOR CORRECTIVE ACTIONS The organization: (a) Measures the time between flaw identification and flaw remediation.
SI-2(3)(b)	FLAW REMEDIATION | TIME TO REMEDIATE FLAWS / BENCHMARKS FOR CORRECTIVE ACTIONS The organization: (b) Establishes [Assignment: organization-defined benchmarks] for taking corrective actions.

SP 800-53 Control Item	Control Text
SI-2(5)	FLAW REMEDIATION | AUTOMATIC SOFTWARE / FIRMWARE UPDATES The organization installs [Assignment: organization-defined security-relevant software and firmware updates] automatically to [Assignment: organization-defined information system components].
SI-2(6)	FLAW REMEDIATION | REMOVAL OF PREVIOUS VERSIONS OF SOFTWARE / FIRMWARE The organization removes [Assignment: organization-defined software and firmware components] after updated versions have been installed.
SI-3(4)	MALICIOUS CODE PROTECTION | UPDATES ONLY BY PRIVILEGED USERS The information system updates malicious code protection mechanisms only when directed by a privileged user. [MAPCAT-ACPR]
SI-3(6)(a)	MALICIOUS CODE PROTECTION | TESTING / VERIFICATION The organization: (a) Tests malicious code protection mechanisms [Assignment: organization-defined frequency] by introducing a known benign, non-spreading test case into the information system.
SI-3(6)(b)	MALICIOUS CODE PROTECTION | TESTING / VERIFICATION The organization: (b) Verifies that both detection of the test case and associated incident reporting occur.
SI-3(7)	MALICIOUS CODE PROTECTION | NONSIGNATURE-BASED DETECTION The information system implements nonsignature-based malicious code detection mechanisms.
SI-3(8)	MALICIOUS CODE PROTECTION | DETECT UNAUTHORIZED COMMANDS The information system detects [Assignment: organization-defined unauthorized operating system commands] through the kernel application programming interface at [Assignment: organization-defined information system hardware components] and [Selection (one or more): issues a warning; audits the command execution; prevents the execution of the command].
SI-3(9)	MALICIOUS CODE PROTECTION | AUTHENTICATE REMOTE COMMANDS The information system implements [Assignment: organization-defined security safeguards] to authenticate [Assignment: organization-defined remote commands].
SI-3(10)(a)	MALICIOUS CODE PROTECTION | MALICIOUS CODE ANALYSIS The organization: (a) Employs [Assignment: organization-defined tools and techniques] to analyze the characteristics and behavior of malicious code.

SP 800-53 Control Item	Control Text
SI-3(10)(b)	MALICIOUS CODE PROTECTION | MALICIOUS CODE ANALYSIS The organization: (b) Incorporates the results from malicious code analysis into organizational incident response and flaw remediation processes.
SI-7(3)	SOFTWARE, FIRMWARE, AND INFORMATION INTEGRITY | CENTRALLY-MANAGED INTEGRITY TOOLS The organization employs centrally managed integrity verification tools.
SI-7(6)	SOFTWARE, FIRMWARE, AND INFORMATION INTEGRITY | CRYPTOGRAPHIC PROTECTION The information system implements cryptographic mechanisms to detect unauthorized changes to software, firmware, and information.
SI-7(8)	SOFTWARE, FIRMWARE, AND INFORMATION INTEGRITY | AUDITING CAPABILITY FOR SIGNIFICANT EVENTS The information system, upon detection of a potential integrity violation, provides the capability to audit the event and initiates the following actions: [Selection (one or more): generates an audit record; alerts current user; alerts [Assignment: organization-defined personnel or roles]; [Assignment: organization-defined other actions]].
SI-7(9)	SOFTWARE, FIRMWARE, AND INFORMATION INTEGRITY | VERIFY BOOT PROCESS The information system verifies the integrity of the boot process of [Assignment: organization-defined devices].
SI-7(10)	SOFTWARE, FIRMWARE, AND INFORMATION INTEGRITY | PROTECTION OF BOOT FIRMWARE The information system implements [Assignment: organization-defined security safeguards] to protect the integrity of boot firmware in [Assignment: organization-defined devices].
SI-7(11)	SOFTWARE, FIRMWARE, AND INFORMATION INTEGRITY | CONFINED ENVIRONMENTS WITH LIMITED PRIVILEGES The organization requires that [Assignment: organization-defined user-installed software] execute in a confined physical or virtual machine environment with limited privileges.
SI-7(12)	SOFTWARE, FIRMWARE, AND INFORMATION INTEGRITY | INTEGRITY VERIFICATION The organization requires that the integrity of [Assignment: organization-defined user-installed software] be verified prior to execution.

SP 800-53 Control Item	Control Text
SI-7(13)	SOFTWARE, FIRMWARE, AND INFORMATION INTEGRITY	CODE EXECUTION IN PROTECTED ENVIRONMENTS The organization allows execution of binary or machine-executable code obtained from sources with limited or no warranty and without the provision of source code only in confined physical or virtual machine environments and with the explicit approval of [Assignment: organization-defined personnel or roles].
SI-7(15)	SOFTWARE, FIRMWARE, AND INFORMATION INTEGRITY	CODE AUTHENTICATION The information system implements cryptographic mechanisms to authenticate [Assignment: organization-defined software or firmware components] prior to installation.
SI-7(16)	SOFTWARE, FIRMWARE, AND INFORMATION INTEGRITY	TIME LIMIT ON PROCESS EXECUTION W/O SUPERVISION The organization does not allow processes to execute without supervision for more than [Assignment: organization-defined time period].
SI-14	NON-PERSISTENCE Control: The organization implements non-persistent [Assignment: organization-defined information system components and services] that are initiated in a known state and terminated [Selection (one or more): upon end of session of use; periodically at [Assignment: organization-defined frequency]].
SI-14(1)	NON-PERSISTENCE	REFRESH FROM TRUSTED SOURCES The organization ensures that software and data employed during information system component and service refreshes are obtained from [Assignment: organization-defined trusted sources].

Appendix E. SWAM-Specific Acronyms and Abbreviations*

DLL	Dynamic Link Library
SWID	Software Identification
TPM	Trusted Platform Module

*Note that acronyms common to multiple capabilities are addressed in Volume 1 of this NISTIR.

Appendix F. Glossary

Core Software	An organizationally defined set of software that, at a minimum, includes firmware and root operating system elements used to boot the system. Core software merits specialized monitoring as it may be difficult for commonly used whitelisting software to check.
Cryptographic Hash Value	The result of applying a cryptographic hash function to data (e.g., a message). (Source: SP 800-57).[28] Also see Message Digest.
Digital Fingerprint	See Message Digest.
Digital Signature	An asymmetric key operation where the private key is used to digitally sign data and the public key is used to verify the signature. Digital signatures provide authenticity protection, integrity protection, and non-repudiation, but not confidentiality protection. (Source: SP 800-63).[29]
Installation (as used herein)	Any of the following actions: • Executing an installer to load software. • Listing software in the operating system software directory • (Merely) placing executable software files on a medium from which it can be executed, even if no installer software is run and there is no listing for it in the operating system software directory. • Any other action that allows an executable software file to be loaded into the CPU (e.g., browsing a website that downloads software; opening an e-mail (or attachment) that downloads software; etc.)
Message Digest	The result of applying a hash function to a message. Also known as a "hash value" or "hash output". (Source: SP 800-107).[30] A digital signature that uniquely identifies data and has the property that changing a single bit in the data will cause a completely different message digest to be generated. (Source: SP 800-92).[31]

---

[28] https://doi.org/10.6028/NIST.SP.800-57pt1r4
[29] https://doi.org/10.6028/NIST.SP.800-63-3
[30] https://doi.org/10.6028/NIST.SP.800-107r1
[31] https://doi.org/10.6028/NIST.SP.800-92

	A cryptographic checksum, typically generated for a file that can be used to detect changes to the file. Synonymous with hash value/result. (Source: CNSSI-4009).[32]
SWID Tag	A SWID tag is an ISO 19770-2 compliant XML file describing a software product. It is typically digitally signed by the software manufacturer to verify its validity. Ideally, for purposes of software asset management, the SWID tag will contain the digests (digital fingerprints) of each software file installed or placed on the device with the product.
Zero-Day Attack	An attack that exploits a previously unknown hardware, firmware, or software vulnerability.

---

[32] https://www.cnss.gov/CNSS/issuances/Instructions.cfm

Appendix G. Control Items Affecting Desired and/or Actual State from All Defect Checks in this Volume

This table is to support root cause analysis when a specific defect check fails. Such a failure might be caused not only by a failure of the specific control items mapped to that defect check in the defect check narratives, but also by a failure in any of the following control items. As used here, these controls apply to potential defects in the desired state (DS) and/or actual state (AS). The rationale column explains how a defect in the control item might cause the defect check to fail.

Note: These items are not explicitly included in the control item assessment narratives, unless they also apply to CM of items other than the desired and actual states, *for assessment.*

Determination Statement ID	Determination Statement Text	Impact Level	Affects DS and/or AS	Rationale
CM-2{1}	Determine if the organization: develops, documents, and maintains under configuration control, a current baseline configuration of the information system.	Low	DS	Otherwise, there is no desired state for testing.
CM-2(1)(a){1}	Determine if the organization: reviews and updates the baseline configuration of the information system: (a) [Assignment: organization-defined frequency].	Moderate	DS	Otherwise, the desired state might not be updated as needed to maintain appropriate security.
CM-2(1)(b){1}	Determine if the organization: reviews and updates the baseline configuration of the information system: (b) When required due to [Assignment organization-defined circumstances].	Moderate	DS	Otherwise, desired state might not be updated based on the organization-defined circumstances.
CM-2(1)(c){1}	Determine if the organization: reviews and updates the baseline configuration of the information system: (c) As an integral part of information system component installations and upgrades.	Moderate	DS	Otherwise, desired state might not be updated as appropriate when component installations and updates occur.

Determination Statement ID	Determination Statement Text	Impact Level	Affects DS and/or AS	Rationale
CM-2(2){1}	Determine if the organization: employs automated mechanisms to maintain an up-to-date, complete, accurate, and readily available baseline configuration of the information system.	High	DS	Otherwise accurate testing information might not be provided.
CM-3(a){1}	Determine if the organization: employs automated mechanisms to determine the types of changes to the system {installed software} that are configuration-controlled.	Moderate	DS	Otherwise, the desired state might not specify all {machine-readable} data needed for implemented defect checks.
CM-3(b){1}	Determine if the organization: reviews proposed configuration-controlled changes to the {software of the} system and approves or disapproves such changes.	Moderate	DS	Otherwise, the decisions on desired state might not adequately reflect security impact of changes.
CM-3(b){2}	Determine if the organization: explicitly considers security impact analysis when reviewing proposed configuration-controlled changes to the {software of the} system.	Moderate	DS	Otherwise, the decisions on desired state might not adequately reflect security impact of changes.
CM-3(c){1}	Determine if the organization: documents configuration change decisions associated with the system {installed software}.	Moderate	DS	Otherwise changes to the desired state specification might not be documented and available {as machine-readable data}.
CM-3(d){1}	Determine if the organization: implements approved configuration-controlled changes to the system {installed software}.	Moderate	AS	Otherwise, defect checks might fail because changes were not implemented in the actual state.
CM-3(f){1}	Determine if the organization: audits activities associated with configuration-controlled changes to the {software of the} system.	Moderate	DS	Otherwise, errors in the desired state might not be detected.
CM-3(f){2}	Determine if the organization: reviews activities associated with configuration-controlled changes to the {software of the} system.	Moderate	DS	Otherwise, errors in the desired state might not be detected.

Determination Statement ID	Determination Statement Text	Impact Level	Affects DS and/or AS	Rationale
CM-3(g){1}	Determine if the organization: coordinates configuration change control activities {of software} through [Assignment: organization-defined configuration change control element (e.g., committee, board)] that convenes [Selection (one or more): [Assignment: organization-defined frequency]; [Assignment: organization-defined configuration change conditions].	Moderate	DS	Otherwise, the persons authorized to make change approval decisions, and the scope of their authority, might not be clearly defined to enable knowing what decisions are authorized.
CM-3(g){2}	Determine if the organization: provides oversight for configuration change control activities {of software} through [Assignment: organization-defined configuration change control element (e.g., committee, board)] that convenes [Selection (one or more): [Assignment: organization-defined frequency]; [Assignment: organization-defined configuration change conditions].	Moderate	DS	Otherwise, the persons authorized to make change approval decisions, and the scope of their authority, might not be clearly defined to enable knowing what decisions are authorized.
CM-3(1)(a){1}	Determine if the organization: employs automated mechanisms to document proposed changes to the system {installed software}.	High	DS	Otherwise changes to the desired state specification might not be documented and available for assessment.
CM-3(1)(b){1}	Determine if the organization: employs automated mechanisms to notify [Assignment: organized-defined approval authorities] of proposed changes to the system {installed software} and request change approval.	High	DS	Otherwise, needed changes might not be reviewed in a timely manner.
CM-3(1)(c){1}	Determine if the organization: employs automated mechanisms to highlight proposed changes to the system {installed software} that have not been approved or disapproved by [Assignment: organization-defined time period].	High	DS	Otherwise, needed changes might not be reviewed in a timely manner.

Determination Statement ID	Determination Statement Text	Impact Level	Affects DS and/or AS	Rationale
CM-3(1)(d){1}	Determine if the organization: employs automated mechanisms to prohibit changes to the system {installed software} until designated approvals are received.	High	DS	Otherwise, unapproved changes might be implemented.
CM-3(1)(e){1}	Determine if the organization: employs automated mechanisms to document all changes to the system {installed software}.	High	AS	Otherwise, documented changes might not reflect the actual state of the system.
CM-3(1)(f){1}	Determine if the organization: employs automated mechanisms to notify [Assignment: organization-defined personnel] when approved changes to the system {installed software} are completed.	High	DS	Otherwise, required changes might be missed.
CM-3(2){1}	Determine if the organization: tests, validates, and documents changes to the {software of the} system before implementing the changes on the operational system. Not applicable in the operational environment. This should be assessed via manual reauthorization prior to placing policy in the desired state. Because it occurs as part of system engineering, it is outside the scope of this operational capability.	Moderate	DS and AS	Otherwise, changes might increase risk by creating operational or security defects.
CM-8(a){1}	Determine if the organization: develops and documents an inventory of system components {for software} that: (1) accurately reflects the current system; and (2) includes all components within the authorization boundary of the system.	Low	DS and AS	Otherwise the desired state and actual state inventories might have errors related to accuracy, completeness, and/or content.

Determination Statement ID	Determination Statement Text	Impact Level	Affects DS and/or AS	Rationale
CM-8(a){2}	Determine if the organization: develops and documents an inventory of system components {for software} that is at the level of granularity deemed necessary for tracking and reporting [by the organization].	Low	DS and AS	Otherwise the desired state and actual state inventories might have errors related to level of detail.
CM-8(b){1}	Determine if the organization: updates the system component inventory {for software} [Assignment: organization-defined frequency].	Low	DS and AS	Otherwise, defects in the desired state and actual state inventories, and related processes, might not be detected.
CM-8(b){2}	Determine if the organization: reviews the system component inventory {for software} [Assignment: organization-defined frequency].	Low	DS and AS	Otherwise, defects in the desired state and actual state inventories, and related processes might not be detected.
CM-8(1){1}	Determine if the organization: updates the inventory of system {installed software} components as an integral part of component installations, removals, and system updates.	Moderate	DS and AS	Otherwise, defects in desired state and actual state inventories and related processes might not be detected.
CM-8(2){1}	Determine if the organization: employs automated mechanisms to help maintain an up-to-date, complete, accurate, and readily available inventory of system {installed software} components.	High	DS and AS	Otherwise, an up to date and accurate desired state and actual state inventories might not be available for automated assessment.
CM-8(3)(a){1}	Determine if the organization: employs automated mechanisms [Assignment: organization-defined frequency] to detect the presence of unauthorized software and firmware components within the system.	Moderate	AS	Otherwise, inventory accuracy (e.g., completeness and timeliness) might be difficult or impossible to maintain.

Determination Statement ID	Determination Statement Text	Impact Level	Affects DS and/or AS	Rationale
CM-8(3)(b){1}	Determine if the organization: takes the following actions when unauthorized {installed software} components are detected: [Selection (one or more): disables network access by such components; isolates the components; notifies [Assignment: organization-defined personnel or roles]].	Moderate	AS	Otherwise, detected security defects might not be mitigated.
CM-8(4){1}	Determine if the organization: includes in the {installed software} system component inventory information, a means for identifying by [Selection (one or more): name; position; role], individuals responsible/accountable for administering those components.	High	DS	Otherwise, when defects are detected, the automated systems cannot know what persons or groups to notify to take appropriate action.

Control Allocation Table for Appendix G [a]

Determination Statement ID	Implemented By	Assessment Boundary	Assessment Responsibility	Assessment Methods	Selected	Rationale for Risk Acceptance	Frequency of Assessment	Impact of Not Implementing	Level
CM-2{1}	DSM	ISCM-TN	ISCM-Sys	Test					Low
CM-2(1)(a){1}	DSM	ISCM-TN	ISCM-Sys	Test					Moderate
CM-2(1)(b){1}	DSM	ISCM-TN	ISCM-Sys	Test					Moderate
CM-2(1)(c){1}	DSM	ISCM-TN	ISCM-Sys	Test					Moderate
CM-2(2){1}	DSM	ISCM-TN	ISCM-Sys	Test					High
CM-3(a){1}	DSM	ISCM-TN	MAN	TBD					Moderate
CM-3(b){1}	DSM	ISCM-TN	ISCM-Sys	Test					Moderate
CM-3(b){2}	DSM	ISCM-TN	MAN	TBD					Moderate
CM-3(c){1}	DSM	ISCM-TN	ISCM-Sys	Test					Moderate
CM-3(d){1}	SWMan	ISCM-TN	ISCM-Sys	Test					Moderate
CM-3(f){1}	ISCM-Sys	ISCM-TN	ISCM-Sys	Test					Moderate
CM-3(f){2}	DSM	ISCM-TN	ISCM-Sys	Test					Moderate
CM-3(g){1}	DSM	ISCM-TN	ISCM-Sys	Test					Moderate
CM-3(g){2}	DSM	ISCM-TN	ISCM-Sys	Test					Moderate
CM-3(1)(a){1}	DSM	ISCM-TN	ISCM-Sys	Test					High
CM-3(1)(b){1}	ISCM-Sys	ISCM-TN	ISCM-Sys	Test					High
CM-3(1)(c){1}	ISCM-Sys	ISCM-TN	ISCM-Sys	Test					High
CM-3(1)(d){1}	ISCM-Sys	ISCM-TN	ISCM-Sys	Test					High
CM-3(1)(e){1}	ISCM-Sys	ISCM-TN	MAN	TBD					High
CM-3(1)(f){1}	ISCM-Sys	ISCM-TN	ISCM-Sys	Test					High
CM-3(2){1}	DSM	ISCM-TN	MAN	TBD					Moderate
CM-8(a){1}	DSM	ISCM-TN	ISCM-Sys	Test					Low
CM-8(a){2}	ISCM-Sys	ISCM-TN	ISCM-Sys	Test					Low
CM-8(b){1}	ISCM-Sys	ISCM-TN	ISCM-Sys	Test					Low
CM-8(b){2}	DSM	ISCM-TN	ISCM-Sys	Test					Low

AUTOMATION SUPPORT FOR SECURITY ASSESSMENTS: SWAM

Determination Statement ID	Implemented By	Assessment Boundary	Assessment Responsibility	Assessment Methods	Selected	Rationale for Risk Acceptance	Frequency of Assessment	Impact of Not Implementing	Level
CM-8(1){1}	ISCM-Sys	ISCM-TN	ISCM-Sys	Test					Moderate
CM-8(2){1}	ISCM-Sys	ISCM-TN	ISCM-Sys	Test					High
CM-8(3)(a){1}	ISCM-Sys	ISCM-TN	ISCM-Sys	Test					Moderate
CM-8(3)(b){1}	SWMan	ISCM-TN	ISCM-Sys	Test					Moderate
CM-8(4){1}	DSM	ISCM-TN	ISCM-Sys	Test					High

[a] The control allocation table is provided as a partially completed security assessment plan template. Organizations may leverage the template by documenting organization- and/or system-specific information in the blank columns..

www.ingramcontent.com/pod-product-compliance
Lightning Source LLC
Chambersburg PA
CBHW080409060326
40689CB00019B/4180